W9-BIR-110

As Fresh as it Gets

As Fresh as it Gets

Everyday Recipes from the Tomato Fresh Food Café

Christian Gaudreault and Star Spilos

ARSENAL PULP PRESS

VANCOUVER

AS FRESH AS IT GETS
Copyright © 2006 by Christian Gaudreault and Star Spilos

Second printing: 2006

All rights reserved. No part of this book may be reproduced or used in any form
by any means—graphic, electronic or mechanical—without the prior written
permission of the publisher, except by a reviewer, who may use brief excerpts in a
review, or in the case of photocopying in Canada, a license from Access Copyright.

ARSENAL PULP PRESS
341 Water Street, Suite 200
Vancouver, BC
Canada V6B 1B8
arsenalpulp.com

The publisher gratefully acknowledges the support of the Government of Canada
through the Book Publishing Industry Development Program for its publishing
activities.

The authors and publisher assert that the information contained in this book is
true and complete to the best of their knowledge. All recommendations are made
without guarantee on the part of the author and Arsenal Pulp Press. The authors
and publisher disclaim any liability in connection with the use of this information.
For more information, contact the publisher.

Text design and cover design by Electra Design Group
Production assistance by Diane Yee
Photography by Bryan Ponsford
Food styling by Maurizio Peta
Editing by Melva McLean with Brian Lam and Nicole Marteinsson

PRINTED AND BOUND IN CHINA

Library and Archives Canada Cataloguing in Publication

Gaudreault, Christian, 1950–
      As fresh as it gets : everyday recipes from the Tomato Fresh Food
Café / Christian Gaudreault and Star Spilos.

Includes index.
ISBN 1-55152-199-7

      1. Cookery. 2. Tomatoes—History. 3. Tomato Fresh Food Café.
I. Spilos, Star, 1956– II. Title.
TX714.G37 2006   641.5   C2006-900711-X

ISBN-13: 978-155152-199-2

Contents

ACKNOWLEDGMENTS

Writing a cookbook was a dream we had that was made a reality by many supportive and talented people. First we must give a huge thanks to Melva McLean for recognizing that our vision for this cookbook had great potential. With her encouragement, she helped us make this possible. Our chef, James Campbell, produces amazing food at the Tomato every evening and continually wows us with his talent; thanks to him and his awesome kitchen team, including sous chef Joe Wight, who are all talented in their own right. A special thanks to our pastry chef Jennifer Lee for all her help with recipe testing and to all our managers and the front staff for their loyalty and dedication.

Thanks to photographer Brian Ponsford without whose beautiful photographs this book would not be complete, and food stylist Maurizio Peta for his amazing eye and creativity. Thanks also to John and Jason Puddifoot for providing us with dishes for the photos. To Susan Davidson and everyone at Glorious Garnish and Seasonal Salad Co. and Glen Valley Organic Farm Co-Operative: our gratitude for sharing your beautiful farms and the stories behind the organic produce we all enjoy. We also appreciate all of our other suppliers who are dedicated to providing us (and others) with excellent product and service. To Dawn Kelly and Diane Clement for the recipes, and to Carole Jackson and my sister Carell Bayne for being there to help. Thanks to the team at Arsenal Pulp Press for your support, talent, and belief in the Tomato Fresh Food Café. And finally, to all our customers who support us: a big thank you.

FOREWORD

by Diane Clement

It's hard to believe that in 1991 we opened the doors to the Tomato Fresh Food Café in Vancouver with my daughter Jennifer and partners Haik Gharibians and Jamie Norris. The neighborhood welcomed us with open arms, raving about our "fresh food concept." In 1995, we launched the first Tomato cookbook, *Diane Clement at the Tomato*. At the same time, we decided to seek a general manager for the restaurant. Christian lived in the neighborhood and he and his wife Star both were loyal "Tomato" fans; one morning, Christian walked in for his usual coffee and casually mentioned to Jennifer and me that he was interested in the position. The rest is history.

With his strong background in the food industry, and with the same vision, passion, and dedication as we had, Christian soon became a partner, as well as a friend. The restaurant soon expanded, taking over the grocery store next door, and grew from 45 seats to 100. In the spring of 2001, Jennifer and I felt it was time to pass on the "baton" to Christian. Talented Chef James Campbell, a Maritimer like me, now spearheads the strong Tomato kitchen team, and many of the dedicated staff that was with us when we left are still there, and key to the Tomato's continued success. What is rewarding to me is the fact that the Tomato Fresh Food Café is as popular as ever. Christian grew up learning his craft in his father's restaurant in Cap de la Madeleine, Quebec, and I know that his parents would be as proud of him as Jennifer and I are to see the Tomato Fresh Food Café mature to become one of Vancouver's best-loved restaurants. Congratulations, Christian and Star, on the birth of *As Fresh As It Gets*, the latest addition to the Tomato family.

INTRODUCTION

by Star Spilos

It's the first of October, but the sun is shining. Christian and I wander the market in our T-shirts, even though the chill in the air, and the falling leaves—with their beautiful shades of red and gold—tell us that it won't be long before the cold, rainy weather sets in. We can look forward to only one more Saturday at the Trout Lake Farmer's Market in East Vancouver before the season is over. Going to this popular, well-organized market is one of the highlights of our week. We enjoy seeing the abundance of local farm fresh products, much of it organically grown; we also visit artisans selling pottery and jewelry, and stop by booths offering homemade chocolates and specialty cheeses. We wish these weekly trips to the market would never end, but now the weather is changing, the crops are not as plentiful, and the farmers are looking tired, so we try to make the most of our day.

As Christian and I do on every visit, we pick up Sieglinde potatoes from Doug and Jeanette Helmer of Helmer's Organic Farm in Pemberton, BC. Kevin and Annamarie Klippenstein, who own Klippers Organic Acres—growers of the heirloom tomatoes we receive—have a new apple called Mutsu (or Crispin) to show us. We stop to talk to Susan Davidson of Glorious Garnish and Seasonal Salad Company; just days earlier, she delivered the last twelve pounds of scarlet runner beans of the season to our restaurant. We chat about the difference between white turnips and yellow rutabaga, and buy some of her delicious arugula.

It's not uncommon to see chefs from several Vancouver restaurants at the market looking for special seasonal items for their menus. In fact, on this day we see several chefs who are simply there to answer questions from customers about how to use particular ingredients.

Christian and I find a great selection of squash today. We buy a huge, 40-pound Blue Hubbard variety, along with several others, from the Forstbauer Family Natural Food Farm. The squash will make a great display at the entrance to our restaurant. We end our day at the market by ordering artichokes for pick-up the following week, and purchasing some great breads and pastries from a talented baker, Christopher Brown of Rise Bakery. Now it's time to go home with all our purchases: local, fresh ingredients "from the farmer's fields to our table," as Christian likes to say.

Our home is our restaurant, the Tomato Fresh Food Café, located at the corner of 17th Avenue and Cambie Street in Vancouver. It first opened in August 1991, but its history goes back to 1947 when it was the site of a diner called the Rosebud Grill. In those days, Jersey Dairy, which produced most of the milk consumed in Vancouver, was located right next door. Families living in the Cambie Corridor (as the area is still called) went to the dairy on warm summer days to get fabulous ice cream.

Some time in the late 1950s or early 1960s, the Rosebud Grill became the Sun Ray Grill. A small part of the front was partitioned off to create a barbershop, where Charlie, the barber, still works to this day. In 1991, the neighborhood, and the unique character of the 1940s building, attracted the attention of the founding partners of the Tomato Fresh Food Café: Diane Clement, Jennifer Clement, Jamie Norris, and Haik Gharbians. They maintained the restaurant's original booths and counter and created what became a neighborhood institution, where people could gather to share good conversation and healthy food; where young and old could sit next to each other and talk over a bowl of homemade soup.

Christian joined the Tomato in 1995 as a partner and general manager, and led the way to its expansion in 1997. When Dave's, the little grocery store next door, gave up its lease, the Tomato took the opportunity to "grow around the barber." The café grew into a "big" Tomato with 100 seats, a new bar, and a take-out service, Tomato To Go, located at the front of the restaurant. This also made room for a bakery, where the café's desserts and breads are made and sold. Over the years, there were other changes: Haik sadly passed away, then Jamie decided to leave to become a full-time writer. In May 2000, Diane retired to travel with her husband Doug, and their daughter Jennifer left to put more time into her acting career. That's when Christian and I became the proud sole owners.

Food and family have always played a major role in both our lives. Aime Gaudreault, Christian's father, was a chef in Cap de la Madeleine, Quebec. The entire Gaudreault clan—Christian's mother Germaine, and his five brothers and five sisters—worked in the family restaurant. One of the highlights of Aime's culinary life came in 1944, at the Château Frontenac hotel in Quebec City. The event was a meeting to plan D-Day; in attendance were Canadian Prime Minister William Lyon Mackenzie King, US President Franklin D. Roosevelt, and British Prime Minister Winston Churchill. At the formal dinner, Aime served the head table. A photograph showing him with these world leaders still hangs in the gift shop at the hotel, and a copy of the menu remains a Gaudreault family treasure. Christian's mother was also a great cook; she instilled in Christian the importance of getting food from the farm to the table as soon as possible. The Gaudreaults' passion for food was truly part of the family's everyday lives at work and at home. For Christian, the social interaction that brings family and friends together around the dining table holds great importance, whether it is at home or at the Tomato.

The idea of putting fresh food on the table has always been in my family too. My family always had a garden; we planted vegetables, fruit, and herbs to be used in our cooking and we eagerly anticipated using these fresh ingredients in our meals. My mother often used the apples and raspberries from the backyard for our evening dessert. My father was the gardener of the family; every year he had a contest with the neighbors as to who could grow the biggest beefsteak tomato. All summer, they would inspect each other's gardens to see who was going to win, but the real prize was eating them! My sister (also named Carell) shares the family passion for food; she lives in Delta, British Columbia and has continued the family tradition of keeping a wonderful garden, from which she gathers ingredients to make the most delicious dinners.

As a young adult, Christian began exploring the hospitality opportunities of Europe. He also spent time in Morocco, India, Indonesia, and the Philippines, where he was amazed by the huge papayas, the rice patties that spread from the mountains down to the valley, and the mangos, which remain the best he's ever tasted. (He also got a bit role as a co-pilot in the 1979 film *Apocalypse Now*.) Moving to Vancouver in the 1970s, Christian worked under famed chef and restaurateur Umberto Menghi. He was also the sales and marketing director of Yves Veggie Cuisine, and general manager of Caper's restaurants, before we became owners of the Tomato.

I worked at Kelly Douglas & Company, a wholesaler grocer, for sixteen years. Dad worked for the same company his entire working life, forty-three years—and my mother did as well for a time, doing food demos. In 1996, Les Dames d'Escoffier awarded me a scholarship to further my culinary expertise in pastry at the Culinary Institute of America-Napa Valley. Previous to this honor, I studied at the Dubrulle French Culinary School in Vancouver, and assisted chef Ann Willan on her PBS television series

John Switzer of Glen Valley Organic Farm Co-operative, with Christian and Star.

Look and Cook. (This would later lead to a job assisting with the preparation of the food used onscreen for the Robin Williams movie *Jumanji*.) My first job after completing school was at Sweet Obsession Cakes and Pastries, where the owners reinforced my belief that only the best ingredients should be used and that shortcuts did not necessarily produce quality goods. Yet early in my career I wanted my own business, so I started my own company Starbake, selling biscotti to various cafés in the city.

For the past ten years, I have worked at David Thompson Secondary School in Vancouver, instructing and supervising students in food handling and the preparation of baked goods. Since 1997, I also have been involved with the bakery at the Tomato, where we produce the pastries, desserts, and most of the breads we serve and sell.

Owning a restaurant is not a job; it is a passion. It is the love of food, people, and the challenges we face each day. There's a terrific amount of detail that goes into running a restaurant, from sourcing product to maintaining equipment to hiring staff. It takes lots of energy, dedication, and determination. The restaurant is forever changing—whether it is exciting new ingredients to use, or the menus that change with each new season. Our neighborhood evolves and changes too: some favorite merchants nearby close, but new ones open; familiar customers move away, but new regulars abound. A restaurant becomes part of the surrounding community; as we support them, they support us.

The Tomato is a warm, simple room with lots of energy. It's a neighborhood restaurant where people come to enjoy wonderful meals, whether they relax alone with a cup of coffee, or share a laugh with family and friends. The staff always looks forward to seeing the regular customers as well as welcoming first-timers. And we are long-time supporters of our local farmers, sourcing out organic produce whenever possible and using seasonal ingredients.

There's a reason for this. Over the years, food has changed because we now know more about what's good for us. Customers no longer want their food laden with heavy sauces, and they know the importance of eating lots of vegetables and fruit. Food must be creative yet simple and good for you. At the Tomato, we use some of the best local food suppliers around.

Christian and Chef James always attend the "Chefs to the Field," an annual fundraiser held at the Glen Valley Organic Farm every August. This event draws many food lovers and chefs out of their kitchens and into the garden to experience the full cycle of food. Each attending chef creates a dish using what is at its peak in the garden at the time of the event. They then compete for the Green Cuisine Culinary Award, a contest in which they prepare a dish with one ingredient of their choice and one surprise protein. Proceeds from this event help the Glen Valley Organic Farm and Fraser Common Farm, where the Glorious Salads are cultivated. The goal of these farms is to protect and steward land by keeping it out of the speculative real estate market and allowing organic farmers to have affordable access through lease arrangements.

It's this sense of responsibility and connection to the earth that we try to bring to the Tomato. On a typical weekend in late summer, Christian and I often show up at the restaurant with produce fresh from the farmer's market—potatoes, peppers, corn, heirloom tomatoes. Chef James Campbell has to be flexible when we arrive with produce that's just been picked from the field; he adjusts the evening meal to accommodate seasonal produce. In a restaurant, the kitchen is an intense environment where speed and timing are crucial. It is vital that everyone in the kitchen works harmoniously together and Chef James has the kind of leadership to motivate the staff to produce their best work. We all share the same vision for the Tomato, and continue to learn and grow together to ensure that customers always leave with smiles on their faces. This passion for food, our passion for life, and our commitment to our staff and our customers make for a successful and special restaurant.

Which brings us to *As Fresh As It Gets*. This book is about the Tomato Fresh Food Café, but it's also about the two of us, our discovery of the world of food, and the contribution of our family, friends, and community to who we are today. Writing it has been hard work but also a lot of fun. We hope it gets your culinary juices flowing, and introduces you to the importance of fresh, local, socially responsible food, from the farmer's fields to your dinner table.

Breakfast and Brunch

Breakfast Scramble

Zucchini & Eggplant Omelet

Poached Eggs on English Muffins with
European Back Bacon

Christian's Tomato, Red Pepper, Asparagus
& Gruyère Frittata

Tomato, Chorizo & Manchego Frittata

Crispy Bacon, Gruyère & Spinach Quiche

Three-cheese Strata

Tofu Scramble with Salsa

Dave's Blackberry Mascarpone French Toast
with Caramelized Apples

Buttermilk Cornmeal Pancakes

Yogurt Cheese

French Breakfast

Sun-dried Cranberry Pecan Granola

Breakfast Drinks:
Suzy Q
Whammy
Veg Head
Heavenly Cleanse
Guiltless Chocolate Banana Tofu Smoothie
Raspberry Retreat

At home, weekends give us a break from our busy daily routines and offer us time to relax and linger over the first meal of the day. Breakfast and brunch are an often overlooked opportunity to casually entertain family and friends. We often start such meals with a freshly-squeezed juice. A healthy alternative is the Veg Head (page 31), but for a tasty and nutritious treat you'll have to try the Guiltless Chocolate Banana Tofu Smoothie (page 32).

Frittatas and quiches are versatile egg dishes to make when entertaining at breakfast or brunch. Two of our favorite frittatas are Christian's Tomato, Red Pepper, Asparagus & Gruyère (page 22), and for meat lovers, the Tomato, Chorizo & Manchego (page 23). Don't overlook the simpler egg recipes like the Zucchini & Eggplant Omelet (page 20) or the Breakfast Scramble (page 19). Of course, any egg dish relies on good quality ingredients, like the Omega-3 eggs we get from Kidd Bros. Look for suppliers in your area.

If you want a change from eggs, try the Tofu Scramble (page 26), the Buttermilk Cornmeal Pancakes (page 28), or the Sun-Dried Cranberry Pecan Granola (page 30). You also can check out the Baking chapter for muffins and scones, which make easy and quick breakfast treats.

BREAKFAST SCRAMBLE

Here's a great weekend breakfast you can make with the kids. To save time, chop all the vegetables the evening before and keep them in the refrigerator overnight. Chefs call ahead-of-time preparation *mise en place*, which means "setting in place."

2 tbsp olive oil or butter
¾ cup zucchini, finely chopped
½ cup yellow bell peppers, seeded and finely chopped
1 tsp jalapeño pepper, seeded and finely chopped (see note)
1 clove garlic, finely chopped
3 large eggs
2 tbsp milk
¼ cup Parmesan or medium Cheddar cheese, grated
pinch of salt
freshly ground pepper to taste

- In a large non-stick frying pan on medium heat, heat the oil or butter and sauté the zucchini, peppers, jalapeño, and garlic for 2 minutes, until vegetables are tender.

- In a medium bowl, beat the eggs, milk, cheese, salt, and pepper together until blended.

- Pour into the frying pan with the vegetables and cook on medium heat for 2 minutes. Stir the mixture around with a spatula until eggs begin to set. Serve immediately.

Makes 2 servings.

Good quality jalapeño peppers should be green with firm, smooth skins. Dry lines are not blemishes; they are signs of a mature pepper and indicate a hot taste. When handling peppers remember to wash your hands afterwards, and avoid touching your eyes. The dried form of the jalapeño is called a chipotle pepper.

ZUCCHINI & EGGPLANT OMELET

The simplest egg dish can often be difficult to prepare well, but with a few tips and good organization, it can be done with ease. Before you start an omelet, have your ingredients prepared and ready to use. Make each omelet separately, just like we do at the café.

1 to 2 tbsp olive oil
½ cup eggplant, diced
½ cup zucchini, diced
1 small tomato, diced
3 large eggs
1 tbsp milk
salt and freshly ground pepper to taste
1½ tsp butter
⅓ cup Gruyère cheese, grated

- In a medium frying pan on medium heat, sauté the eggplant and zucchini in oil for 3 minutes. Add the tomatoes and cook for an additional minute, or until the zucchini and eggplant are tender. Remove vegetables from pan and set aside.

- In a medium bowl, beat the eggs, milk, salt, and pepper together until blended.

- Using the same frying pan on medium heat, add the butter to coat the surface of the pan.

- Pour the egg mixture into the pan. When the mixture starts to cook, use a spatula to lift the edge of the cooked egg and tip the pan to allow the uncooked egg to run underneath.

- At the moment the eggs are no longer liquid but still are glossy on top, place the grated cheese and vegetables on one side of the omelet. Using the spatula, fold the other side of the omelet over the vegetables and cheese.

- Gently slide the omelet onto a plate and serve immediately.

Makes 1 omelet.

POACHED EGGS ON ENGLISH MUFFINS WITH EUROPEAN BACK BACON

A poached egg is one of those comfort foods that can start the day just right. Here's a simple method that works every time. We serve this dish with Roasted Sieglinde Potatoes (page 111) and salad greens.

4 slices European back bacon (see note)
pinch of salt
1 tbsp white vinegar
4 large eggs
2 English muffins, toasted and cut in half

- In a frying pan on medium-high heat, fry the back bacon on both sides
- Fill a deep-sided skillet or pan with water at least 3 inches deep. Add a pinch of salt and bring to a boil
- Reduce heat to simmer and add the vinegar.
- Swirl the water with a slotted spoon and then crack the eggs into the moving, swirling water. This method keeps the eggs from sticking to the bottom of the pan.
- Cook to your preference: soft poached – 2 minutes; medium poached – 3 minutes, and hard poached – 4 minutes.
- Remove each egg with a slotted spoon.
- Serve each egg on half of an English muffin topped with a slice of back bacon.

Makes 4 servings.

European back bacon is a much leaner type of bacon and goes perfectly with poached eggs, but you can use your favorite bacon in this recipe.

CHRISTIAN'S TOMATO, RED PEPPER, ASPARAGUS & GRUYÈRE FRITTATA

A frittata is a simple and tasty dish to make for your weekend brunch. You can use a variety of cheeses and different vegetables. Try using Omega-3 eggs, which are lower in cholesterol than normal ones because the chickens are fed a special diet. The addition of baking powder makes the frittata light and fluffy.

1 tbsp olive oil
3 Roma tomatoes, cubed
1 small red bell pepper, seeded and cubed
6 asparagus spears, cooked and cut in 1-inch pieces
salt and freshly ground pepper to taste
8 large eggs
½ cup milk
1 cup Gruyère cheese, grated
½ tsp baking powder

- Preheat oven to 375°F (190°C).
- In a large non-stick, ovenproof frying pan on medium heat, heat the oil and sauté the tomatoes, red peppers, and asparagus for 3 minutes. Season with salt and pepper.
- In a medium bowl, beat the eggs, milk, cheese, and baking powder until blended. Pour into the frying pan. Transfer pan to oven and bake for 18 minutes.

Makes 3–4 servings.

TOMATO, CHORIZO & MANCHEGO FRITTATA

The Tomato goes through 2,500 eggs every weekend. Here's a variation on the previous frittata recipe.

1 chorizo sausage (wine-cured is best)
1 tbsp olive oil
3 Roma tomatoes, cubed
salt and freshly ground pepper to taste
8 large eggs
½ cup milk
1 cup Manchego cheese, grated (see note)

- Preheat the oven to 375°F (190°C).

- In a medium frying pan on medium heat, fry the chorizo sausage. Once cooked, slice and drain on a paper towel.

- In a large non-stick, ovenproof frying pan, heat the oil and sauté the tomatoes for 5 minutes. Add the sausage and season with salt and pepper.

- In a large bowl, beat the eggs, milk, and cheese. Pour into the frying pan. Transfer pan to oven and bake for 18 minutes

Makes 3–4 servings.

Manchego cheese is available in specialty cheese shops and gourmet grocers. Gruyère, Monterey Jack, or cheddar cheese would make good substitutes.

CRISPY BACON, GRUYÈRE & SPINACH QUICHE

Every lunchtime at the café, we make this quiche with a variety of fillings that reflect the seasons. In spring, we use asparagus; in summer, zucchini and tomato; in fall, spinach. In winter, we keep it simple yet rich, using mushrooms and extra cheese. Try it with your own favorite seasonal ingredients.

Pastry:

- 1 cup cold butter, cut into small cubes
- 2 ⅔ cups all-purpose flour
- ½ cup ice water

Filling:

- 4 to 5 cups fresh spinach
- 8 to 10 slices side bacon
- 4 large eggs
- 1 ½ cups whipping cream
- 1 tsp salt
- ½ tsp freshly ground pepper
- pinch nutmeg
- 1 cup shredded Gruyère or Swiss cheese
- pinch of freshly ground pepper

- Preheat oven to 350°F (180°C).

- By hand or in a food processor, combine the butter and flour until the butter resembles peas.

- Add ice water and combine until just mixed; form dough into a ball.

- Flatten dough into a disk. Wrap in plastic wrap. Chill at least 30 minutes in the refrigerator.

- Using a rolling pin, roll dough about ¼-inch thick to fit a 9-inch tart pan.

- Par-bake shell for 20 to 25 minutes (you want the pastry to be three-quarters baked) (see note).

- In a saucepan on medium-low heat, sauté the spinach until evenly wilted, about 3 to 4 minutes. Remove any excess water.

- In a medium frying pan on high heat, cook bacon until crispy; pat dry and crumble.

- In a large bowl, beat the eggs, whipping cream, salt, pepper, and nutmeg until blended.

- Add the bacon, cheese, and spinach in the pastry shell. Cover with the egg and cream mixture and season with salt and pepper. Bake for 45 minutes, until set.

Makes 6–8 servings.

When par-baking the pastry shell, line it with foil and then place uncooked beans on top. This prevents the pastry from shrinking. Also, spraying the foil where it touches the pastry will stop the pastry from sticking to the foil.

THREE-CHEESE STRATA

A strata is made with eggs, cheese, cream, and bread, similar to a savory bread pudding. This strata is easy to prepare for a brunch and even better reheated the next day. Serve it on its own or with tossed salad greens.

½ lb asparagus (about 12 spears)
1 cup mushrooms, sliced
½ cup red bell pepper, seeded and chopped
2 tbsp olive oil
1 ½ cups whole milk
6 cups day-old sourdough bread, cut into
    1-inch cubes, crusts removed
1 cup whipping cream
4 large eggs
2 cloves garlic, chopped

½ tsp salt
¼ tsp freshly ground pepper
¼ tsp nutmeg
¼ tsp fresh thyme, stems removed
    and chopped
1 tsp fresh parsley, chopped
½ cup goat cheese, crumbled
¾ cup Parmesan cheese, grated
¾ cup Gruyère cheese, grated

- Preheat oven to 350°F (180°C).

- Butter an 8-inch-round, 3-inch-deep baking dish.

- In a medium saucepan on high heat, blanch the asparagus by boiling for 2 minutes, then plunging into cold water. Cut each spear into 3 pieces.

- In a medium frying pan on medium-high heat, sauté the mushrooms and the red peppers in oil for 5 minutes. Set aside.

- In a large bowl, combine the milk and bread cubes and let sit for 10 minutes, until the liquid is absorbed.

- In a separate bowl, whisk together the whipping cream, eggs, garlic, salt, pepper, nutmeg, thyme, and parsley.

- In a buttered pan, layer strata by placing ½ the bread mixture in the bottom of the baking dish, then ½ the vegetables and ½ the cheese. Repeat layers one more time.

- Pour in the egg mixture.

- Bake uncovered until firm in the center and golden brown, about 1 hour 15 minutes. The strata will rise slightly.

Makes 6–8 servings.

TOFU SCRAMBLE WITH SALSA

Before Christian owned the Tomato Fresh Food Café, he worked for his friend Yves Potvin, who at the time owned Yves Veggie Cuisine. That was the beginning of Christian's love affair with tofu. One day, he tried it in place of eggs and it became this scrambled breakfast favorite.

Scramble:

1 tbsp olive oil

½ cup red bell pepper, seeded and finely diced

½ cup yellow bell pepper, seeded and finely diced

½ cup zucchini, finely diced

⅓ cup red onion, finely diced

½ cup salsa

1 tbsp curry mix (see note)

1 tsp salt

1 tsp freshly ground pepper

16-oz (454-g) pkg medium-firm tofu

Salsa (makes 1 cup):

¼ cup red onion, diced

1 tbsp jalapeño pepper, chopped

1 tbsp lime juice

1 tbsp fresh cilantro leaves

½ tsp salt

½ tsp freshly ground pepper

2 Roma tomatoes, chopped

For the salsa:

- In a food processor, pulse all ingredients except the tomatoes for 20 seconds until fine, then add the tomatoes and pulse for an additional 10 seconds.

- The salsa will keep in the refrigerator for 3 days.

For the scramble:

- In a large non-stick saucepan on medium heat, add the oil and sauté the vegetables for 2 to 3 minutes, or until tender.

- Add the salsa, curry mix, salt, and pepper. Sauté for 1 to 2 minutes, then reduce heat to low.

- Drain the tofu, then crumble into the pan. Cook for 2 to 3 minutes to warm the tofu up. Add salt and pepper to taste.

Makes 4 servings.

The Tomato's Curry Mix

3 tbsp curry powder

2 tbsp turmeric

2 tbsp ground cumin

1 tbsp ground coriander

- Blend all the spices together and store in a jar until needed. Make extra and keep on hand for other curry dishes.

Makes ½ cup.

DAVE'S BLACKBERRY MASCARPONE FRENCH TOAST WITH CARAMELIZED APPLES

If you love breakfast you must come for weekend brunch at the Tomato. Dave Gibbs' Blackberry French Toast with caramelized apples is enough to get anyone to wake up early.

½ cup mascarpone cheese, at room temperature
3 tbsp white sugar
½ cup fresh blackberries
2 Granny Smith apples, peeled and cut into 8 slices each
2 tbsp white sugar (for apples)
¼ tsp cinnamon

2 tbsp butter
3 large eggs
1 tsp white sugar
1 tsp vanilla
¼ tsp cinnamon
⅛ tsp nutmeg
4 slices sourdough bread (each 1 ¼ inches thick)

- To make blackberry mascarpone: mix the cheese (be sure it's at room temperature) and 3 tbsp sugar. Fold in the blackberries and set aside.

- To caramelize apples: in a small frying pan on low heat sauté the apples, 2 tbsp sugar, and cinnamon in butter until apples are tender, about 5 to 6 minutes. The sugar will caramelize to a light golden brown. Remove from heat and set aside.

- In a medium bowl, beat the eggs, 1 tbsp sugar, vanilla, cinnamon, and nutmeg.

- Slice each piece of sourdough bread down the center to make a pocket. (Do not cut all the way through.)

- Place ¼ of the mascarpone mixture inside each bread pocket.

- Dip both sides of the bread into the egg mixture.

- In non-stick frying pan on medium heat, fry the bread on both sides until golden brown, about 3 to 4 minutes each side.

- Top with the caramelized apples.

Makes 4 servings.

You can prepare the French toast up to and including dipping in the egg mixture. Place in the refrigerator until ready to use.
You can use cream cheese in place of the mascarpone.

BUTTERMILK CORNMEAL PANCAKES

We serve these very popular pancakes as a brunch special. When you make them at home, use a medium to coarsely ground yellow cornmeal. Serve with fresh seasonal berries, yogurt cheese, and a drizzle of maple syrup.

¾ cup all-purpose flour
2 tbsp white sugar
½ cup coarsely ground yellow cornmeal
4 tsp baking powder
½ tsp salt

1 cup buttermilk
⅓ cup butter, melted and cooled
2 eggs, beaten
1 tbsp vegetable oil, for the pan
yogurt cheese (recipe below)

- In a large bowl, mix the flour, sugar, cornmeal, baking powder, and salt.

- In a separate bowl, combine the buttermilk, melted butter, and eggs and mix well.

- Mixing by hand, add the wet ingredients to the dry until the batter is combined. (It will be slightly lumpy.)

- In a lightly oiled skillet on medium heat, pour one ladle of batter at a time and cook until the bubbles break on the surface. Flip and cook the other side until golden brown.

Makes 6–8 pancakes.

YOGURT CHEESE

Unflavored yogurt cheese is so versatile it can be used in any dish in place of sour cream, such as a garnish for soup or a salad dressing. At the Tomato, we flavor the yogurt cheese and serve it with Buttermilk Cornmeal Pancakes (recipe above).

3 cups unflavored natural yogurt
juice of 1 orange
½ cup honey
1 tsp vanilla extract

- Line the inside of a strainer with cheesecloth or a coffee filter.
- Pour the yogurt into the strainer. Place strainer over a large, deep bowl and cover with plastic wrap. Refrigerate for 3 to 24 hours. (The longer it chills, the thicker it will be.)
- Just before serving, mix in the orange juice, honey, and vanilla.
- The yogurt cheese will keep in the refrigerator for up to 1 week.

Makes 1 ½ cups.

FRENCH BREAKFAST

Ooh la la! Filled with fresh fruit, this is a light and nutritious to start your day—a French breakfast!

2 slices white sourdough bread
1 oz raspberry jam
2 oz Brie cheese (1 wedge)
¼ banana, sliced
1 slice each: apple, orange, grapefruit, cantaloupe, honeydew melon, pineapple, and/or other fruit of your choice
3 to 5 each of blackberries, blueberries, and raspberries

- Toast the sourdough bread and slice on diagonal.
- On a plate, arrange the toast, jam, cheese wedge, and sliced fruit.

Makes 1 serving.

SUN-DRIED CRANBERRY PECAN GRANOLA

This granola (inspired by a recipe brought to us by a former chef, Lisa Rowson) is perfect for your power breakfast! It will keep in an airtight container for up to 1 month. Use dried fruit of your choice in place of the cranberries, and add your favorite nuts. Almonds are awesome with sun-dried cranberries.

5 cups old-fashioned rolled oats (see note)
1 cup oat bran
1 cup pecans, chopped
½ cup pumpkin seeds
½ cup honey or pure maple syrup
½ cup canola oil
⅓ cup water
¾ cup coconut
1 cup raisins
¾ cup sun-dried cranberries

- Preheat oven to 300°F (150°C).

- In a large bowl, mix the rolled oats, oat bran, pecans, and pumpkin seeds.

- In a separate bowl, mix the honey, oil, and water.

- Add the dry ingredients to wet and mix well.

- Spread evenly on a cookie sheet and bake, stirring every 15 minutes, until cereal is evenly browned and crunchy, about 35 to 45 minutes.

- Remove from oven. When cooled, add the coconut, raisins, and sun-dried cranberries.

Makes 8 cups.

There are two types of oats commonly available: steel cut oats, also known as "Irish" or "Scottish" oats; and rolled oats, of which there are three varieties: old-fashioned (also known as large flake oats), quick-cooking, and instant oatmeal.

Breakfast Drinks

The Tomato Fresh Food Café was the first restaurant in Vancouver to have a juice bar. As former partner Diane Clement said, "It was a top priority when we opened the café to have freshly squeezed juices." They tested and drank buckets of juice to come up with these recipes; knowing Diane and her daughter Jennifer, they must have had many laughs thinking up the names for these concoctions. Their research has proved to be very good, because after all these years we still have many of them on our Juice Bar List.

For all these juices and smoothies, simply throw the ingredients into a blender and mix until smooth, about 30 seconds.

Suzy Q

This drink is named after Diane Clement's daughter-in-law Suzanne.

1 banana
¼ cup ice
¾ cup freshly squeezed orange juice
½ cup strawberries

Makes 2 servings.

Whammy

A tropical paradise ... a vacation you can drink!

1 banana
¼ cup ice
⅓ cup freshly squeezed orange juice
⅓ cup pineapple juice

Makes 2 servings.

Veg Head

The ultimate healthy drink! This is a way to switch your metabolism into overdrive.

3 medium carrots, roughly chopped
2 stalks celery, roughly chopped
⅛ cucumber
1 tbsp beet juice
1½ tbsp spinach leaves

Makes 2 servings.

HEAVENLY CLEANSE

This is our best-seller: the purifier! Guaranteed to keep you healthy and happy.

- 2 apples, peeled, cored, and roughly chopped
- 3 medium carrots, roughly chopped
- 1 tsp fresh ginger juice
- Juice of ½ lemon

Makes 2 servings.

GUILTLESS CHOCOLATE BANANA TOFU SMOOTHIE

Over the years Christian and I have also experimented with breakfast drinks. This one came about when I met Sally Errey, who encouraged me to have a smoothie made with high-protein tofu in the afternoon before I went out to exercise. I always ate yogurt and chocolate so, I thought, why not put them together? And who doesn't like chocolate and bananas?

- 1 banana
- ½ cup soft tofu
- ½ cup vanilla yogurt
- 2 tbsp good quality cocoa powder
- 2 tbsp honey
- ½ cup ice cubes

Makes 2 servings.

RASPBERRY RETREAT

This one is named after a neighborhood store that always had wonderful work from local artists. Emily, its owner, had amazing energy and community spirit.

- 1 banana
- 2 tbsp raspberries
- ½ cup pineapple juice
- ¼ cup ice

Makes 2 servings.

French Breakfast (page 29)

Sun-Dried Cranberry
Pecan Granola (page 30)

Poached Eggs on English Muffins with European Back Bacon (page 21)

Buttermilk Cornmeal Pancakes with Yogurt Cheese (page 28)

Starters

TOMATO, BOCCONCINI, BASIL & RED ONION SALAD

HEIRLOOM TOMATO SALAD

CHRISTIAN'S SUMMER SALAD WITH CORN,
ARUGULA & FETA CHEESE

THE WESTCOASTER SALAD

ARUGULA, FRESH FIG & CRISPY PROSCIUTTO SALAD

COLESLAW WITH AVOCADO MAYONNAISE DRESSING

POACHED PEAR & PECAN SALAD
WITH WARM GOAT CHEESE

MEDITERRANEAN SALSA

OLIVE TAPENADE

OVEN-ROASTED TOMATOES & FETA ON CROSTINI
WITH INFUSED BASIL OIL

MUSSELS IN WHITE WINE SAUCE

CRAB CAKES WITH DUNGENESS & BLUE CRABMEAT

SAUTÉED PRAWNS WITH FRESH GINGER ORANGE LIME
SAUCE & SESAME OIL SOBA NOODLES

PAN-SEARED SCALLOPS

ASPARAGUS, FETA & PESTO TART

CORN CAKES WITH SMOKY TOMATO SAUCE

FRENCH CANADIAN TOURTIÈRE

A simple salad made with crisp, just-picked organic lettuce or mixed young greens is a great start to any meal. So is a bowl of recently harvested mussels served in a delicately spiced broth, or a plate of corn cakes with a flavorful relish on the side. Appetizers like these, made with the freshest ingredients possible, awaken our appetites and make all of our senses come alive. Whenever I'm served a tasty and beautifully presented appetizer—whether at a restaurant or a friend's house—I look forward with pleasure to the rest of my meal.

Christian and I love summertime when we can go to the market and let the farm fresh produce help us create the salad of the day, but you can serve salads year round as long as you let your choices change with the seasons. Some of our favorites are Christian's Summer Salad with Local Corn, Arugula & Feta Cheese (page 40), Arugula, Fresh Fig & Crispy Prosciutto Salad (page 42), which is a showcase for fall figs, and the Poached Pear & Pecan Salad with Warm Goat Cheese (page 44).

If you want a more substantial appetizer, try the Mussels in White Wine Sauce (page 49) or the Crab Cakes with Dungeness & Blue Crabmeat (page 51). For meat lovers, we are so proud and pleased to share the Gaudreault family recipe for French Canadian Tourtière with Germaine's (Christian's mom) Tomato Fruit Ketchup (page 56).

TOMATO, BOCCONCINI, BASIL
& RED ONION SALAD

This classic Italian dish is very simple, and a great way to feature *summer*-ripened tomatoes and fresh basil from your garden. Be sure to use a good quality extra-virgin olive oil and *balsamic* vinegar. You can split this recipe into individual portions or serve it on one large platter.

4 Roma tomatoes
3 bocconcini rounds (approx. 3 oz each)
6 to 8 fresh basil leaves
¼ red onion, thinly sliced
¼ cup extra-virgin olive oil
2 tbsp balsamic vinegar
salt and freshly ground pepper to taste

- Slice the tomatoes and bocconcini into ¼-inch (6-mm) thick slices.
- Place a slice of tomato on top of each slice of bocconcini, and a basil leaf on top of the tomato. Scatter red onion slices over top. Drizzle with oil and vinegar. Season with salt and pepper.

Makes 4–6 servings.

Bocconcini, originally from Italy, is fresh mozzarella that is stored in water because it is more perishable than regular mozzarella. It's also sweeter and softer, and is mostly used in salads and sandwiches. It comes in rounds about 2 inches in diameter and can be found in Italian markets or specialty grocers.

Heirloom Tomatoes

When I was growing up, my father grew tomatoes in our backyard garden. They tasted like tomatoes should taste: sweet, juicy red, sun-ripened, and bursting with flavor. They were delicious. But I lost my love for tomatoes when, as an adult, I started to buy them at the grocery store; they were flavorless, pale imitations of the real thing. This was before farmer's markets started up in my neighborhood; it was only then that I discovered heirloom tomatoes, which are grown from seeds passed down through the generations. Today, these old varieties are back with a vengeance and widely available. Now I love tomatoes again!

Heirloom tomato aficionados everywhere are introducing people to varieties that haven't been grown in years. In fact, there is so much interest in them that heirloom tomato festivals are being held all over North America. Recently, Christian and I attended a festival at the Kendall Jackson Wine Center in Santa Rosa, California. The festival featured over 200 varieties of heirloom tomatoes picked fresh from their gardens, and we had an opportunity to taste many of them.

Heirloom tomatoes have many different flavors and textures; they also come in a wide range of sizes, shapes, and colors. Some are even multi-colored, like Julia Child's Copia variety, and the Green Zebra, which has green and yellow stripes and a sweet flavor with a tart undertaste. The Black Krim is a large, dark-red fruit with a rich, sweet flavor. Brandywine, a medium-sized fruit with a sweet, slightly spicy flavor, has a thin skin and lots of juice. Tiger Strip, also called Tigerella, is a sweet yet tart tomato with a taste of lemon.

One of my favorite large tomatoes, good for the BLT on page 66, is the oddly-named Radiator Charlie's Mortgage Lifter. Like many heirlooms, this one has an interesting origin. In the 1940s, the owner of a radiator repair shop started growing tomatoes. The shop was located at the foot of a very steep hill in the Appalachian Mountains where trucks would often overheat. The shop owner, known as "Radiator Charlie" experimented by crossing four varieties and coming up with a large pink variety weighing about 2 ½ pounds, which attracted gardeners from miles away. He started to sell seedlings for $1 each; within six years, he had made $6,000 from his seedlings and was able to pay off his mortgage, thus the name of this heirloom: Radiator Charlie's Mortgage Lifter.

So what makes a good tomato? For me, it has to feel heavy in the hand, with a pleasing, pungent aroma and with thin skin that comes off easily when I peel it. When I cut it, it yields willingly beneath a sharp blade without pressure or sawing. Once sliced, its flesh should shine, and the small seed pockets should glisten with thick gel. In my mouth, it feels silky on the tongue and tastes both sweet and acidic. Overall, it should have something called "backyard quality"; that sense that you just walked out into your own garden and picked it straight off the vine.

It's also important to decide what you will do with the tomatoes. Some are good for sauces or salsas, and others are better in salads or for soups, tarts or perhaps in a ketchup recipe, like the one on page 132. Go to your local farmer's markets and talk to different tomato suppliers about their varieties and how to use them best.

A word about storage: tomatoes ripen from the inside out, so the best place to store them is on the kitchen counter in a cool spot — somewhere between 55–70°F (13–21°C). You should never refrigerate them because it destroys the flavor and makes the texture mealy.

HEIRLOOM TOMATO SALAD

This salad is simple and lets the tastes and visual beauty of these tomatoes show through. Heirloom tomatoes, in any combination of colors and irregular shapes you can find, are worth seeking out at the farmer's markets. Save some seeds from the heirlooms you buy and grow your own the following year.

6 ripe heirloom tomatoes of different varieties and colors
¼ cup fresh basil leaves
⅓ cup feta cheese, crumbled
2 tbsp extra-virgin olive oil
2 tsp balsamic vinegar
salt and freshly ground black pepper to taste

- Slice the various tomatoes and place them on a platter or on individual plates.
- Tear the basil leaves and scatter on top of tomatoes. Crumble the feta cheese on top of the tomatoes.
- Drizzle oil and vinegar over top. Season with salt and pepper.

Makes 4–6 servings.

Lettuce and Other Salad Greens

Arugula is also called rocket, and is very popular in salads. It has dark green-lobed leaves and a somewhat nutty flavor.

Belgian endive has smooth, cream-colored, slender leaves with pointed heads and a slightly bitter flavor. The Dutch call Belgian endive "wetloof," which literally means "white leaf."

Butter lettuce has fairly large, loose heads with thick leaves and even, green coloring. It is also called Boston or Bibb lettuce.

Cress comes in many varieties. It is best known as watercress, but there is also peppercress, garden cress, and broadleaf cress. All are known for their sweet, spicy flavors.

Fava tips and **pea tips** are mild in flavor and have buttery textures. Interestingly, these tips are often used as cover crops and add nitrogen and organic matter to the soil.

Frisée has slender curly leaves and is found in salad mixes. A relative of the dandelion, frisée is considered "bitter" and, therefore, helpful with digestion, one reason to eat salad at the beginning of a meal.

Kale comes in many varieties and colors, all with frilly leaves. Kale is at its best during the winter months and has a mild cabbage-like flavor.

Loose leaf lettuce comes in varieties like oak leaf, red leaf, and green leaf, and is a type of lettuce that does not form heads. Instead, they are loosely packed and joined at the stem. Its leaves can be ruffled or smooth, and is has a mild, delicate taste and medium crispness.

Mache or **lamb's lettuce** has small, green, finger-like leaves which are extremely perishable. Also known as corn salad or field salad lettuce, mache has a sweet, mild flavor reminiscent of hazelnuts.

Mizuna is also called "kyona." It has dandelion-like, jagged-edged, tender leaves with a mild, sweet peppery flavor. The mildest of the mustard greens, mizuna has nice crunchy stems.

Mustard greens are a rich dark green color, and when sold fresh, can be used like spinach. The plant itself is a cross between a strain of cabbage and black mustard, which is why these greens have a strong mustard flavor.

Radicchio is a variety of red chicory whose origins are in the Veneto region of Northern Italy. Radicchio has burgundy red leaves with white ribs.

Romaine lettuce is the classic lettuce used in Caesar salads. It has good flavor and crunch plus a good shelf life in the refrigerator. It has long and narrow leaves with firm ribs down their centers. Romaine lettuce is said to have originated on the Aegean island of Cos, which is why it is also known as Cos lettuce.

Shingiku is an Asian green. A member of the Chrysanthemum family, it has delicate fern-like leaves that add a slight "retsina" flavor to a salad.

Spinach has emerald green leaves which are generally oval but sometimes heart-shaped, and a slightly bitter flavor.

Tatsoi is a Chinese green from the cabbage family. It has shiny, dark, spoon-shaped leaves.

Susan Davidson of Glorious Garnish, with Christian

CHRISTIAN'S SUMMER SALAD WITH CORN, ARUGULA & FETA CHEESE

This hearty summer salad is a great showcase for the brilliant colors and fresh flavors of corn, beets, and seasonal salad greens. You can prepare the beets and corn the day before and keep them refrigerated until you are ready to make the salad.

4 small beets
2 ears of corn
1 large bunch of arugula or 3 cups baby greens
½ cup cherry tomatoes
½ cup feta cheese, crumbled
Toasted Sesame Vinaigrette (page 124)
salt and pepper to taste

- In a medium pot of water on high heat bring the beets to a boil. Reduce heat to simmer, and cook until tender. Cool, remove skins, and slice thinly. Set aside.

- In another pot, cook the corn in boiling salted water for 3 minutes. Cool and slice kernels from the cob.

- Wash and dry the arugula or baby greens. In a salad bowl, combine greens with the cherry tomatoes, crumbled feta, and corn. Toss with the Toasted Sesame Vinaigrette.

- Add the beets just before serving. Season with salt and pepper.

Makes 4 servings.

THE WESTCOASTER SALAD

If you've ever met Diane Clement the original owner of the Tomato you know she's energetic and fun. Her warmth and love of food and people always show through. Even though she is no longer at the café, we continue to offer her incredibly popular Westcoaster Salad. It's served warm with a combination of candy salmon and chèvre or goat cheese. It's good as an appetizer or as a meal in itself.

1 lb (450 g) mixed seasonal greens
1 cup red bell peppers, seeded and julienned
1 cup yellow bell peppers, seeded and julienned
8 oz (225 g) goat cheese or chèvre, crumbled
8 oz (225 g) Indian candy salmon (see note)
freshly ground pepper to taste
Maple Balsamic Vinaigrette (page 125)

- Arrange salad greens on individual plates or one large salad bowl along with the peppers and goat cheese.

- Peel the skin off the salmon and cut into ¼-inch thick slices.

- In a sauté pan on low heat, slightly warm the Maple Balsamic Vinaigrette. Add the salmon and then toss with the salad

Makes 6 servings.

Our favorite brand of Indian Candy Salmon is Westcoast Select Sundance. It has been hot smoked in a sweet brine, rolled in peppercorns and contains no artificial color or preservatives.

ARUGULA, FRESH FIG & CRISPY PROSCIUTTO SALAD

Our next-door neighbor Angela has two fig trees in her backyard. In late July and early August each summer, she leaves bowls of perfectly ripe figs on our porch. We eat them for breakfast and all through the day, and at dinnertime we use them to make a sauce for fish or cut them up for salads like this one. The crispy prosciutto adds a dramatic effect.

4 slices of prosciutto, sliced very thin
4 cups arugula
4 fresh figs, quartered
½ cup small cherry tomatoes, halved
extra-virgin olive oil (for drizzling)
balsamic vinegar (for drizzling)
salt and freshly ground pepper to taste
Parmeggiano-Reggiano cheese (for shaving)

- Preheat oven to 250°F (120°C).

- Place the prosciutto slices on a baking tray lined with parchment and cover with another piece of parchment. Place another baking sheet firmly on top to help the prosciutto retain its flat shape. Bake in the oven for 30 minutes, or until crisp.

- In a large bowl, combine the arugula, figs, and cherry tomatoes. Drizzle with oil and vinegar. Season with salt and pepper.

- Arrange salad on individual plates. Using a potato peeler, shave cheese on top of salads, then add a slice of crispy prosciutto.

Makes 4 servings.

There are many types of fresh figs available; all are sweetly fragrant and full of flavor when ripe. The most popular is the mission variety, which is purple black in color, but there are also Calimyrnas figs from California, also known as Smyran from Turkey, which has white flesh and green skin. Brown turkey figs from California are large with brown skin and pink flesh. Choose figs that are ripe to get the best flavors; they are perishable and delicate, and should be stored in the refrigerator for only 2 or 3 days.

COLESLAW WITH AVOCADO MAYONNAISE DRESSING

The tender, crinkly leaves of the Napa cabbage along with the crunchy red cabbage and a creamy dressing accentuated by the soft texture of the avocado makes this an exceptional salad to serve with the Chef's Baby Back Ribs (page 90).

Salad:

2 cups red cabbage

2 cups Napa cabbage

2 large carrots, julienned

3 celery stalks, julienned

½ red bell pepper, seeded and julienned

½ yellow bell pepper, seeded and julienned

Dressing:

1 ripe avocado, mashed

½ cup mayonnaise

¼ tsp salt

freshly ground pepper to taste

- In a food processor or chopped by hand, shred both cabbages, then in a medium bowl, combine with the carrots, celery, and peppers.

- In a separate bowl, mix together the avocado and mayonnaise. Toss vegetables with dressing. Season with salt and pepper.

Makes 4–6 servings.

POACHED PEAR & PECAN SALAD WITH WARM GOAT CHEESE

We created this salad to showcase the baby spinach from Susan Davidson's organic farm and serve it from May to the end of October, when spinach is at its best.

Maple Syrup Candied Pecans:

- ½ cup white sugar
- ¼ cup water
- 1 ½ cups pecan halves
- ¼ cup maple syrup

Port Dressing:

- ¾ cup port
- 2 tbsp honey
- 2 tbsp raspberry vinegar
- ½ cup olive or canola oil

Poached Pears:

- 4 Bosc pears, cored, peeled, and quartered
- 2 cups white wine
- 2 cups water
- juice of 1 lemon
- 1 cinnamon stick

Salad:

- 4 cups fresh baby spinach
- ½ cup port dressing
- 4 poached pears

Breaded Goat Cheese Rounds:

- 8 oz (225g) goat cheese or chèvre
- ½ cup flour
- 2 eggs, beaten
- ½ cup panko crumbs or bread crumbs

For the pecans:

- Preheat oven to 300°F (180°C).
- In a pot on low heat, bring the sugar and water to a boil. Wait until it turns a golden caramel color before removing from heat.
- Add the pecans and maple syrup and mix together well.
- Pour onto a baking sheet and bake for 20 minutes. The sugar will make a candy-like coating on the pecans.
- Cool before using. Stored in a container with a lid, they will last several weeks.

For the pears:

- In a large pot on high heat, bring all ingredients except the pears to a boil.

- Lower the heat and place the pears in the liquid. Gently simmer for 25 minutes until tender. Check for doneness with a paring knife; the pears should still hold their shape, yet not be hard. Set aside to cool.

For the cheese rounds:

- Shape goat cheese into four 2-oz flat round disks.

- Using 3 separate bowls, dredge rounds in the flour, then eggs, and finally the crumbs.

- In a frying pan on medium-high heat, brown the goat cheese rounds on both sides.

- Set aside.

For the dressing:

- In a small pot, reduce port by half.

- In a blender or whisked by hand, combine the other ingredients with port until emulsified.

- This dressing will keep in the refrigerator for 2 weeks.

For the salad:

- Toss the spinach and pears in enough port dressing to coat and divide among the 4 plates, with four ¼ slices of pear per serving.

- Place candied pecans on each plate and top salad with a warm goat cheese round.

Makes 4 servings.

Bosc pears have a sweet tart flavor and work well for this salad because they hold their shape when poached. They are available from October through April. You could also use Bartlet pears, a classic summer pear available July through September. They have juicy, sweet, buttery flesh and skins that turns bright yellow when ripe.

MEDITERRANEAN SALSA

This tangy salsa on top of crostini makes a good appetizer. You also can use it as a garnish for fish. A little bit of this goes a long way in adding flavor.

½ cup Roma tomatoes, diced
½ cup fresh fennel, diced
½ cup red bell pepper, seeded and diced
¼ cup red onion, diced
2 tbsp kalamata olives, pitted and diced
2 tsp capers, rinsed and chopped
1 clove garlic, minced
1 tbsp lemon juice
zest and juice of ½ orange
4 tsp red wine vinegar
3 tbsp extra virgin olive oil
4 tbsp fresh parsley, chopped
2 tbsp fresh basil leaves, chopped
salt and freshly ground pepper to taste

- In a large bowl, toss all the ingredients together.
- This salsa will keep in the refrigerator for up to 1 week.

Makes 6–8 servings.

OLIVE TAPENADE

If you love olives, you'll love this tapenade. It's great served on a toasted baguette or as a spread on a vegetarian sandwich.

1 ½ cups kalamata olives, pitted
2 tbsp capers, drained and rinsed
1 2-oz (55-g) pkg. anchovy fillets, rinsed (optional)
zest of 1 orange, finely chopped
1 tbsp freshly squeezed orange juice
¼ cup parsley
3 cloves garlic
¾ tsp black pepper
¼ cup extra-virgin olive oil

- In a food processor or blender, combine all the ingredients except the oil.

- Slowly pour in the oil while continuing to blend until the tapenade is a smooth paste.

- This tapenade keeps in the refrigerator for 2 to 3 weeks.

Makes 1 ½ cups.

Oven-Roasted Tomatoes & Feta on Crostini with Infused Basil Oil

Infused Basil Oil (makes 1 cup):

◇ 4 oz (225 g) blanched fresh basil leaves
◇ 1 cup olive oil or canola oil

Oven-Roasted Tomatoes:

◇ 6 Roma tomatoes, chopped in half
◇ 3 tbsp virgin olive oil
◇ 1 clove garlic, chopped
◇ 1 tsp fresh thyme, chopped
◇ 1 tsp fresh oregano, chopped
◇ 1 pinch sea salt

Crostini:

◇ 12 fresh basil leaves
◇ ½ baguette, sliced
◇ Infused basil oil (instructions below)
◇ 6 oz (170 g) feta cheese, crumbled

- To blanch basil leaves: place in a pot of boiling water for approximately 10 seconds. Remove immediately and place into an ice bath to cool down quickly.

- Squeeze the excess water from the basil and transfer to a blender. Blend for 1 minute with oil. (Do not over blend or the basil will turn black.) Strain through a fine mesh strainer. The basil oil will keep 4 to 5 days.

- Preheat oven to 350°F (180°C).

- Toss tomatoes with olive oil, garlic, thyme, oregano, and salt.

- Place on a baking sheet and bake for 1 hour and 15 minutes. Remove and let cool.

- Cut half a baguette into 12 thin slices and place on a baking sheet. Bake at 350°F (180°C) for 5 to 6 minutes, or until the baguette is toasted.

- Brush each slice of toast with infused basil oil. On each, place a fresh basil leaf, then an oven-roasted Roma tomato, then a piece of the feta cheese.

Makes 4–6 servings.

Heirloom Tomato Salad (page 37)

Poached Pear & Pecan Salad with Warm Goat Cheese (page 44)

Christian's Summer Salad with Corn,
Arugula & Feta Cheese (page 40)

Arugula, Fresh Fig & Crispy Prosciutto Salad (page 42)

MUSSELS IN WHITE WINE SAUCE

Fresh mussels for sale are kept alive in saltwater tanks. Bring them home and remove any sand with a small brush, then remove the beards by just pulling on them. (The beards are what help the mussel hold on to the rocks.) If any mussels do not open after cooking, they should be discarded. We like to use our local honey mussels or Salt Spring Island mussels. The simplest way to enjoy them is steamed open in a little flavorful broth. This is our basic recipe for mussels, which you could also use for clams. We often add other ingredients like saffron, lemon or orange zest, coconut milk, or a variety of fresh herbs.

¼ cup shallots, minced
2 tbsp olive oil
1 tbsp garlic, minced
2 Roma tomatoes, diced
3 lbs fresh mussels, washed
½ cup dry white wine
2 tbsp butter, unsalted
2 tbsp fresh basil leaves, chopped
salt and freshly ground pepper to taste

- In a large pot on medium-high heat, sauté the shallots in oil until translucent, then add the garlic and tomatoes and sauté for an additional minute.

- Add the mussels and white wine. Cover with lid and let mussels steam for 4 to 5 minutes, or until they have opened up.

- Remove the mussels from the broth with a slotted spoon and arrange in a bowl. Stir the butter into the broth and let it reduce by half, stirring occasionally. The more the liquid reduces, the thicker the sauce will be, and the more intense the flavor will become.

- Once the sauce has thickened, add the basil and season to taste. To serve: pour the broth over the mussels.

Makes 6 servings.

About Mussels

The type and availability of mussels will depend on where you live, but here are some popular varieties:

Blue mussels are widely cultured in eastern North America and are named for their solidly blue-black shells.

Greenshell mussels and **Chilean mussels** are summer and early fall varieties. The greenshells have a striking green color, are quite tasty, and also very large. The Chilean mussel is a relative newcomer and is similar in appearance to the Blue mussel.

Honey mussels are found in the cold waters of the Strait of Georgia on the west coast and have a sweet taste and a honey-colored shell.

Mediterranean mussels are at their sweet, tender best through the summer and are easy to farm. They are raised in suspension cultures.

Salt Spring Island Mussels are harvested off the west coast near Vancouver Island. This farm is the first and only mussel farm to raise them from seed grown by their own algae.

CRAB CAKES WITH DUNGENESS & BLUE CRABMEAT

The secret to making the crispy coating of these two cakes is the panko crumbs. Coarser than most commercial bread crumbs, they can be found in specialty Japanese grocers or gourmet food stores. We serve these crab cakes with Peppercorn Aïoli (page 17).

½ lb (250 g) Dungeness crabmeat, well drained
½ lb (250 g) Blue crabmeat, well drained
1 cup cooked potato, riced (see note)
1 cup panko crumbs
1 tbsp Dijon mustard
1 tsp Worcestershire sauce
1 large egg, beaten
¼ tsp hot sauce
3 tbsp mayonnaise
1 celery stalk, finely chopped
1 green onion, finely chopped
freshly ground pepper to taste
1 cup panko crumbs (for coating)

- Preheat oven to 350°F (180°C).
- In a large bowl, combine crabmeat, riced potato, panko crumbs, mustard, and Worcestershire sauce.
- In a separate bowl, combine the egg, hot sauce, mayonnaise, celery, onions, and pepper. Mix well and add to the crab mixture.
- Form into 2-oz (55-g) crab cakes and coat in additional panko crumbs.
- In a frying pan on medium heat, fry the crab cakes until golden brown. Transfer to a baking sheet and bake for 5 to 7 minutes.

Makes 10 2-oz (50-g) crab cakes.

A ricer is a kitchen utensil that looks like a large garlic press, found in specialty cookware shops. If you don't have one, simply mash the potato.

SAUTÉED PRAWNS WITH FRESH GINGER ORANGE LIME SAUCE & SESAME OIL SOBA NOODLES

You can buy fresh local spot prawns in season or frozen in packages of 20/25 count (meaning there are 20 to 25 headless prawns with their shells on). Once they are thawed, remove the shell, make a slit down the back of the prawn, and remove the dark-colored vein. Rinse the prawns in cold water before using.

Prawns:

2 tbsp olive oil
½ tsp fresh ginger, chopped
20 fresh prawns, 20/25 count
2 tbsp white wine
¼ cup orange juice, freshly squeezed
1 tbsp lime juice, freshly squeezed

Sesame Oil Soba Noodles:

2 cups soba noodles
1–2 tsp sesame oil
1 carrot, grated
salt and freshly ground pepper to taste

- In a large skillet on medium-high, heat the oil. Sauté the ginger and prawns for 2 to 3 minutes. Add the white wine and cook for an additional minute.

- Add the orange and lime juices and cook until the sauce just starts to thicken, about 2 to 3 minutes.

- In a large pot of boiling salted water, cook the soba noodles until al dente, about 4 to 5 minutes.

- Drain and toss immediately in sesame oil, coating noodles well.

- Stir in the carrots. Season with salt and pepper.

Makes 4 servings.

PAN-SEARED SCALLOPS

Fresh scallops are available at many fishmongers and markets, but individually frozen ones are available at most grocery stores. They come in a variety of sizes; we like to source the largest ones we can find, which are usually the Atlantic variety. Depending on the size, run 2 to 3 scallops per person; if buying frozen, thaw in the fridge overnight. On the side of each scallop is a little strip called the "tender"; remove it, as it is very tough. Serve these scallops with Wild Mushroom Risotto (page 118) and drizzle with Parsley Scallion Oil (page 126).

16 large scallops
Salt and freshly ground pepper to taste
2 to 3 tbsp olive oil

- Pat scallops dry to remove excess moisture. Season with salt and pepper.
- In a medium skillet on medium-high, heat the oil. Pan sear the scallops until medium rare, about 2 to 3 minutes per side. They should be golden brown in color.

Makes 4 servings.

ASPARAGUS, FETA & PESTO TART

This savory tart makes an impressive brunch when paired with a salad (especially one with arugula, avocado, and pear). On their own, these tarts are great starters for an elegant meal. This recipe uses feta cheese and Traditional Basil Pesto, but the variations are endless; try chanterelle mushrooms sautéed with proscuitto or ham, a tablespoon of cream, and salt and pepper. Another good combination is tomato and bocconcini, with olive paste brushed on top of the puff pastry before baking. Caramelized onions with goat cheese would be delicious. You can find puff pastry in the freezer section of your local grocery store or favorite bakery.

1 12 × 15-inch sheet of puff pastry
24 small to medium asparagus spears, trimmed
½ cup Traditional Basil Pesto (page 136)
½ cup feta cheese, crumbled
2 to 3 tbsp olive oil

- Preheat oven to 400°F (200°C).
- Cut the puff pastry into eight individual triangles that are each about 7 ½ × 3 inches.
- In a pot of boiling salted water, blanch the asparagus for 2 minutes then place into ice water bath to stop the cooking process. Strain to remove any excess water.
- Place the pastry triangles on a baking sheet. Spread 1 tbsp of pesto on each.
- Place 3 asparagus spears on each tart and top with feta. Drizzle 1 tsp olive oil on each tart.
- Bake for 18 to 20 minutes, or until golden brown.

Makes 8 tarts.

CORN CAKES WITH SMOKY TOMATO SAUCE

This dish uses the flavors of New Mexico and makes an excellent starter for entertaining a large group. The Corn Cakes are small and the Smoky Tomato Sauce can be passed around as a dip. The Corn Relish (page 120) goes great with them.

Corn Cakes:

1 ½ cups fresh or frozen corn niblets
    (see note)
1 egg
⅓ cup buttermilk
4 tsp butter, melted
1 green onion, finely chopped
¼ cup coarse cornmeal
1 cup all-purpose flour
½ tsp salt
½ tsp sugar
1 tsp baking powder
⅛ tsp cayenne pepper
vegetable oil (for frying)

Sauce:

1 cup tomato sauce
1 ½ tsp smoked paprika
½ tsp ground chili powder

- To make the sauce: mix all the ingredients together. Set aside.

- Preheat oven to 350°F (180°C).

- In blender or food processor, purée the corn, egg, and buttermilk, allowing the corn to remain a bit chunky.

- Transfer mixture to a bowl and stir in the melted butter and green onions.

- In a separate bowl, combine all the dry ingredients, then add to the liquid ingredients, mixing until blended.

- In a deep-sided skillet or pan, add ½ inch of oil and place on medium-low heat. The oil will be the correct temperature when a droplet of water sizzles in it.

- Place heaping tablespoonfuls of the batter—5 or 6 at a time—into the oil, turning the corn cakes over when lightly browned. (Reduce the heat if they brown too quickly.)

- Place the corn cakes on a baking tray and bake for 5 to 6 minutes until they puff up.

Makes 6–8 servings.

If using fresh corn, boil on the cob for 2 minutes before removing the kernels. If using frozen, thaw before using.

FRENCH CANADIAN TOURTIÈRE

Tourtière is a French Canadian tradition served during winter. The Gaudreault family always serves this dish at Christmas time with their mom's (Germaine's) Tomato Fruit Ketchup. Christian's sister André recently reminded me that when they were kids, because their family was so large – 10 children – they would make five tourtières at one time. Every Christmas Eve, the whole family would come over to celebrate, and the tourtières would be served either before the turkey dinner or alone with vegetables and a salad as a meal in itself. Here is the Gaudreault family version of French Canadian Tourtière.

1 quiche pastry (page 24)
1 small onion, diced
2 tbsp olive oil
½ lb (225 g) ground pork
½ lb (225 g) ground veal
½ cup water
½ tsp dried sorrel
½ tsp salt
½ tsp pepper
½ cup bread crumbs
Germaine's Tomato Fruit Ketchup (page 132)

- Preheat oven to 350°F (180°C).

- Prepare the pastry, place in pie shell, and chill.

- In a frying pan on medium heat, sauté the onions in oil for 2 minutes.

- In a large bowl, mix the remaining ingredients together except the bread crumbs.

- Add the meat mixture to the onions. Reduce heat to low and cook for 20 minutes. Remove from heat.

- Add the bread crumbs and allow to rest for 10 minutes to absorb the moisture.

- Place the cooled mixture into the pastry shell. Cover the top with another layer of pastry and cut slits in the top to let steam out.

- Bake for 40 to 45 minutes, until the crust is golden brown.

- Serve with Germaine's Tomato Fruit Ketchup.

Makes 1 9-inch pie.

Soups, Sandwiches & Burgers

Heirloom Tomato Gazpacho

Babi's Chickpea Potato Soup

Vegetarian Split Pea Soup

Roasted Winter Squash Soup with Pomegranate
Crème Fraîche

My Sister's Chicken Noodle Soup

Joe's Clam Chowder

Tomato Fresh Food Café Heirloom BLT Sandwich

Vegetarian Sandwich

Tomato To Go Three-cheese & Basil Panini

Oven-roasted Lemon Rosemary
Chicken Sandwich

Italian Countryside Sandwich

Italian Panini

Montreal Corned Beef Reuben Sandwich

Portobello Burger

Moroccan Turkey Burger

Soups, sandwiches, and burgers are the cornerstones of our lunch menu at the Tomato. Every day we make two different soups from scratch; soups are a wonderful way to incorporate fresh, healthful ingredients in our diet. We have many regular customers at lunchtime, including Jack, who is 96 years old; he comes all the way across town at least once a week to have a bowl of soup for lunch.

Soup is traditional comfort food—we can all remember at least one favorite our moms used to make. Before the age of instant packaged soups, kitchens were filled with the rich fragrance of fresh ingredients simmering slowly on the back of the stove. Vegetables in season make the best soup ingredients, and in this chapter we offer four vegetarian recipes, including Babi's Chickpea Potato Soup (page 60) and Roasted Winter Squash Soup (page 62). I'm also pleased to give you My Sister's Chicken Noodle Soup (page 63), and a clam chowder (page 64) from Joe, the Tomato's sous-chef.

At the café, we also take sandwiches seriously. We believe a good sandwich starts with great bread, whether it's sourdough or a French baguette, Rosemary Parmesan Focaccia (page 144) or Whole Wheat (page 143). Like the Heirloom Tomato Gazpacho (page 59), the Tomato Fresh Food Café Heirloom Tomato BLT (page 66) are made better by using heirloom tomatoes, which you can read about in detail on page 36. Other sandwich favorites include the Montreal Corned Beef Reuben (page 72) and the Oven-Roasted Lemon Rosemary Chicken Sandwich (page 69).

Like our sandwiches, our burgers are never served with fries but with local organic greens. Two favorites—with both adults and children—are the Portobello Burger (page 73) and the Moroccan Turkey Burger (page 74).

HEIRLOOM TOMATO GAZPACHO

An heirloom tomato is one that has been grown from seeds passed down through several generations, or a variety that is at least 50 years old. You can make this soup even more beautiful by using a variety of different colored tomatoes; try yellow, orange, and green as well as the usual red. Each color has a slightly different flavor. If heirlooms are not available, make this soup with vine-ripened tomatoes.

2 lbs (1 kg) heirloom tomatoes, diced
1 large cucumber, diced
½ cup red onion, finely diced
1 jalapeño pepper, seeded and diced
2 cloves garlic, finely chopped
2 tbsp fresh mint, chopped
2 tbsp fresh basil leaves, chopped
2 cups tomato juice
juice of 1 lime
salt and freshly ground pepper to taste

- In a large bowl, reserve one-third of the tomatoes and cucumber.

- In a food processor, combine remaining tomatoes and cucumber with the red onions, jalapeño, garlic, mint, and basil, and pulse until the mixture is smooth and no large chunks remain.

- Add mixture, along with the tomato juice and lime juice, to the bowl of reserved tomatoes and cucumber. Season with salt and pepper.

- Refrigerate for at least 1 hour before serving.

Makes 4 servings.

BABI'S CHICKPEA POTATO SOUP

Baljinder, or Babi as we know her, has worked with us for eight years; many of us attended her wedding and excitedly awaited the birth of her first child, a daughter. She has always worked in the kitchen, but over time she's started to cook. She is now known for her warm, satisfying soups like this one.

3 tbsp oil
1 large onion, diced
1 tbsp garlic, chopped
1 tbsp fresh ginger, chopped
1 jalapeño pepper, seeded and diced
1 ½ tsp cumin
1 tbsp turmeric
1 tbsp coriander
2 fresh Roma tomatoes, diced
2 tbsp tomato paste
1 potato, peeled and diced
1 14-oz (400-ml) can chickpeas (garbanzo beans)
1 bay leaf (optional)
4 to 5 cups vegetable stock or water
½ cup fresh cilantro leaves, loosely packed
1 tsp salt
½ tsp freshly ground pepper

- In a large pot on medium-low, heat the oil and sauté the onions, garlic, ginger, and jalapeño until they begin to soften, about 5 minutes. Add all the spices and cook for an additional 3 minutes.

- Stir in the tomatoes, tomato paste, potatoes, chickpeas, bay leaf, vegetable stock, and cilantro and simmer for 20 minutes. Season with salt and pepper.

- Remove bay leaf before serving.

Makes 4 servings.

VEGETARIAN SPLIT PEA SOUP

This is a comforting split pea soup without the traditional ham. Make lots; it's great for freezing. Just thaw as needed and add water if it's too thick. You also can make this soup with yellow split peas and two cups of cubed leftover chicken for a variation.

1 large onion, chopped
2 tbsp olive oil or unsalted butter
5 to 6 small potatoes, diced
2 to 3 medium carrots, diced
2 stalks celery, finely chopped
2 cloves garlic, minced
½ tsp fresh oregano
1½ tsp salt
1 tsp pepper
2 cups dry split green peas, rinsed
1 bay leaf
8 to 10 cups vegetable stock or water

- In a large pot on medium heat, sauté the onions in oil, stirring occasionally, until soft.

- Add the potatoes, carrots, celery, garlic, oregano, salt, and pepper. Sauté for an additional 10 minutes, then add the split peas, bay leaf, and vegetable stock.

- Bring to a boil, reduce heat, and let simmer for 40 minutes, or until split peas are soft. Skim off the foam while cooking and stir frequently to avoid burning on the bottom of the pot. Add additional water or stock if the soup is too thick. Adjust seasoning to taste.

- Remove bay leaf before serving.

Makes 6 servings.

ROASTED WINTER SQUASH SOUP WITH POMEGRANATE CRÈME FRAÎCHE

Chef James Campbell made this soup at a recent cooking demonstration at Urban Fare, one of Vancouver's most popular gourmet markets. The crème fraîche has to be made the day before. For more information on winter squashes, see page 115.

3 lbs kuri squash (or your favorite winter squash)
1 medium onion, diced
2 tbsp olive oil
6 cloves garlic, roasted
pinch of cinnamon

pinch of nutmeg
4 cups vegetable stock
salt and freshly ground pepper to taste
pomegranate seeds (for garnish)

- Preheat oven to 350°F (180°C).

- Cut squash lengthwise and scoop out seeds. Roast on a baking sheet, skin side up, for 25 to 30 minutes, or until tender. Let squash cool, remove the skin, and dice flesh.

- In a stockpot on medium heat, sauté onions in oil until softened. Add baked squash, garlic, cinnamon, nutmeg, vegetable stock, salt, and pepper. Bring to a boil, then reduce heat and simmer for 20 to 25 minutes. Adjust seasoning to taste.

- Remove from heat. Carefully pour hot soup into a blender and purée (be careful when blending hot liquids).

- Garnish each bowl with a few pomegranate seeds and a dollop of crème fraîche (see below).

Makes 6 servings.

CRÈME FRAÎCHE

1 cup whipping cream
1 tbsp buttermilk

- Combine cream and buttermilk and pour into a glass jar. Cover and let stand at room temperature for 8 to 24 hours to thicken. Chill for several hours before using.

MY SISTER'S CHICKEN NOODLE SOUP

My sister Carell (who has the same name as my mother) is the soup master. She transforms various vegetables from her garden into a warm and satisfying meal, whether it's a summer garden vegetable soup or a winter soup filled with chicken, egg noodles, and vegetables. Here is her version of chicken noodle soup.

1 medium onion, diced
2 tbsp olive oil
2 medium celery stalks, diced
2 medium carrots, diced
6 cups chicken stock
2 cups water
1 bay leaf
6 oz (170 g) egg noodles
3 cooked chicken breasts, diced
¾ cup fresh or frozen peas
salt and freshly ground pepper to taste

- In a large pot on medium heat, sauté the onions in oil for 3 minutes.
- Stir in the celery and carrots and cook for an additional 3 minutes. Add the chicken stock, water, and bay leaf.
- Increase heat and bring to a boil, add the egg noodles, then reduce heat to medium. Cook for an additional 10 minutes, until the noodles are done and the vegetables are tender.
- Add the cooked chicken and peas just before serving and cook for 2 minutes.
- Remove the bay leaf and season with salt and pepper.

Makes 8–10 servings.

These days, you can purchase good quality, organic chicken broth in containers or tetra packs from most grocery stores.

JOE'S CLAM CHOWDER

Our sous-chef, Joe Wight, is originally from Annapolis Royal near Digby, Nova Scotia, where the economy is based on seafood. Although this is a clam chowder, you could also make this with lobster, white fish, or scallops. In Nova Scotia, Joe used a local wine from Grand Pré Vineyards. Here in Vancouver, we use white wine from the Okanagan Valley in British Columbia. As for the clams, we use local Manila or Savory Island varieties, but you can use any of the four varieties described on the following page.

4 lbs (1 ½ kg) fresh clams or 1 20-oz (560-g) can clams
½ cup dry white wine
6 small potatoes
8 cups chicken stock
1 large onion, diced
3 stalks celery, diced
3 medium carrots, diced
2 medium red bell peppers, seeded and diced
½ cup unsalted butter
2 tbsp fresh thyme, leaves only
2 tsp ground coriander
2 cloves garlic, minced
½ cup flour
2 cups half-and-half cream, 10 % milkfat
1 bay leaf
salt and freshly ground pepper to taste

- If using fresh clams: In a large pot, steam the clams in white wine for about 8 minutes until shells open (discard any that have not fully opened). Remove clams from the shell and set aside.

- Add the potatoes and steam for 20 minutes or until tender. Let cool, then dice.

- In a separate pot on medium-high heat, bring the chicken stock to a simmer.

- In a large saucepan on medium heat, sauté onions, celery, carrots, and red peppers in ½ cup unsalted butter for about 8 minutes. Add the thyme, coriander, and garlic and sauté for another 2 minutes.

- Slowly sprinkle in the flour, stirring into the vegetable mixture to thicken. Let cook for about 5 minutes, then add the hot chicken stock slowly, stirring constantly to remove any lumps.

- Add the clams (if using canned, add clam juice as well), potatoes, cream, and bay leaf. Simmer for another 20 minutes. Remove bay leaf and season with salt and pepper before serving.

Makes 6–8 servings.

Tomato, Bocconcini, Basil & Red Onion Salad (page 35)

Babi's Chickpea Potato Soup (page 60)

Pan-Seared Scallops (page 53)
with Wild Mushroom Risotto (page 118)

Crab Cakes with Dungeness & Blue Crabmeat (page 51)

Clams

Fresh clams, still alive in their shells, are always superior to canned or bottled, whether simply steamed or used in a chowder. Here are a few varieties available at the fishmonger, depending on where you live.

Manila clams are very tender and sweet (although they are rarely eaten raw), and very consistent in size and plumpness. Farmed in Japan for centuries, they were accidentally introduced to the west coast of the US in the 1930s. Today, most Manila clams in the market come from cultured beds in the waters off Washington State. In British Columbia, Manilas are cultured and collected from wild beds, where they are harvested with hand rakes.

Quahog clams are hard-shelled clams found along the east coast. They range in size from ½ inch to 6 inches across. The clams known as Cherrystones and Littlenecks are actually Quahogs, just smaller in size. (There also is a west coast clam called the Littleneck but it is a different species entirely.) The larger, full-sized Quahogs are sometimes called chowder clams, because they can be tough and are best when chopped up and cooked.

Savoury Island clams were also originally from Japan and unintentionally introduced (likely by ballast water) in British Columbia's Strait of Georgia during the late 1980s or early 1990s. With its attractive dark mahogany "finish," this clam reaches 2 ¾ inches (69 mm) in size and is widely found on the beaches along the Strait of Georgia and Northern Puget Sound. It also has been found in Clayoquot and Nootka Sounds in British Columbia and several other locations where other clams are sparsely represented.

Surf clams are the most common east coast species. They also are known as sea clams, skimmer clams, or chowder clams. They are large and comparatively tough, and are most commonly chopped up and used in soups. Most surf clams are canned.

TOMATO FRESH FOOD CAFÉ HEIRLOOM BLT SANDWICH

Summer brings tasty, juicy tomatoes straight from the garden (a bit of salt always brings out their flavor). When we first started using heirloom tomatoes, we got them from our friend Carole, who grew them as a hobby in Vernon, BC. Now we get them from a farm in the Okanagan Similkameen called Klippers Organic Acres; we pick them up at the local farmer's market twice a week. Klippers grows 37 different varieties. Each week, we use 10 or 12, starting in early August and ending in October; some might include: Old Wyamette, Brandywine, COPIA, Julia Child, Green Zebra, Hillbilly, Radiator Charlie's Mortgage Lifter, Paul Robeson, Pegs Round Orange, Pink Pear, Tigerella and Tangello, Black Krim, Green Grape, and Purple Prince. The flavors and colors of these tomatoes make this sandwich stand out. Serve it with organic salad greens and a simple dressing on the side.

4 to 5 slices natural maple-smoked bacon
2 slices sourdough bread, toasted
2 tbsp Homemade Mayonnaise (page 128)
3 large slices of an heirloom tomato
1 or 2 leaves Boston leaf lettuce
salt and freshly ground pepper to taste

- Preheat oven to 400°F (200°C).

- In a shallow baking pan, bake natural maple-smoked bacon for 10 to 20 minutes. Pat dry with paper towel.

- Spread mayonnaise on both slices of toasted sourdough bread.

- Assemble sandwich by layering the heirloom tomatoes, lettuce, and bacon between two slices of bread.

Makes 1 sandwich.

VEGETARIAN SANDWICH

During the day, we offer the Tomato To Go takeout service at the café where people can order soups, sandwiches, and baked goods. This is the first of several fast, delicious, and incredibly satisfying sandwich ideas.

2 slices multi-grain bread
2 tbsp Walnut Hummus (page 135)
1 ½ tbsp Homemade Mayonnaise (page 128)
1 large lettuce leaf
4 slices tomato
4 to 5 slices cucumber
¼ cup carrot, shredded
2 thin slices red onion
1 to 2 slices cheddar cheese
salt and freshly ground pepper to taste

- Spread hummus on one slice of bread; spread the mayonnaise on the other.
- Assemble sandwich by layering remaining ingredients between slices of bread.

Makes 1 sandwich.

Tomato To Go Three-Cheese & Basil Panini

A delicious take on the grilled cheese sandwich.

1 6-inch square of Rosemary Parmesan Focaccia (page 144)
3 tbsp Red Pepper Mayonnaise (page 130)
1 slice each Swiss, cheddar, and fontina cheese
3 to 4 fresh basil leaves

- Slice the focaccia square in half lengthwise and spread mayonnaise on both sides.

- Assemble sandwich by layering remaining ingredients between slices of bread.

- Place on a panini grill or in a frying pan on medium heat. Press top of the grill downward to compress the sandwich or grill until cheese is melted and bread is slightly browned and crisp.

Makes 1 sandwich.

OVEN-ROASTED LEMON ROSEMARY CHICKEN SANDWICH

A great way to use up leftover chicken from your dinner the night before. You can also use rotisserie chicken from your local deli.

⅓ of a French baguette
1 tbsp Dijon mustard
1 tbsp Homemade Mayonnaise (page 128)
1 large leaf lettuce
2 to 3 slices tomato
3-oz Oven-Roasted Lemon Rosemary Chicken (page 85) or cooked chicken of your choice
salt and freshly ground pepper to taste

- Slice the baguette in half diagonally. Combine the mustard and mayonnaise and spread on both sides of bread.

- Assemble sandwich by layering remaining ingredients between slices of bread. Season with salt and pepper.

Makes 1 sandwich.

ITALIAN COUNTRYSIDE SANDWICH

⅓ of a French baguette
2 tbsp Red Pepper Mayonnaise (page 130)
¼ cup watercress
3 to 4 slices tomato
1 ball fresh bocconcini, cut in 4 slices
3 thin slices prosciutto, to taste
salt and freshly ground pepper

- Slice the baguette in half diagonally. Spread mayonnaise on both sides of the bread.
- Assemble sandwich by layering remaining ingredients between slices of bread. Season with salt and pepper.

Makes 1 sandwich.

ITALIAN PANINI

- 1 6-inch square of Rosemary Parmesan Focaccia (page 144)
- 2 tbsp Red Pepper Mayonnaise (page 130)
- 3 to 4 slices tomato
- 1 ball fresh bocconcini, cut in 4 slices
- 3 to 4 leaves fresh basil
- 3 thin slices prosciutto

- Slice the focaccia in half lengthwise and spread mayonnaise on both sides.

- Assemble sandwich by layering remaining ingredients between slices of bread.

- Place on a panini grill or in a frying pan on medium heat. Press top of the grill downward to compress the sandwich or grill until cheese is melted and bread is slightly browned and crisp.

Makes 1 sandwich.

Montreal Corned Beef Reuben Sandwich

Christian is from Cap de la Madeleine in Quebec. Every time he goes back to visit family, he stops in Montreal at Schwartz's delicatessen (a tradition there since 1930) where they serve the best smoked meat sandwiches. Vancouverites love our version, which we serve with organic greens and a dill pickle.

1 tbsp Homemade Mayonnaise (page 128)
1 ½ tsp Dijon mustard
2 slices light rye bread, toasted
4 oz (120 g) Montreal smoked meat
2 oz (60 g) sauerkraut
1 slice Swiss cheese

- Combine the mayonnaise and mustard and spread on both slices of rye bread.
- Assemble sandwich by layering remaining ingredients between slices of bread.

Makes 1 sandwich.

PORTOBELLO BURGER

Our mushroom supplier, Richmond Specialty Mushroom Farms, also sells its products at the farmer's market on weekends, but nowadays portobellos (among other mushrooms) are widely available in grocery stores. Great roasted or grilled, these popular mushrooms are a relative of the fully mature brown crimini and button varieties. They have been called the vegetarian steak for their meaty texture and flavor. Choose mushrooms that are firm and solid to the touch and discard the stems, as they are woody and tough.

2 cloves garlic, finely chopped
¼ cup olive oil
4 large portobello mushrooms, stems removed
salt and freshly ground pepper to taste
4 to 6 oz goat cheese
¼ cup Red Pepper Mayonnaise (page 130)
4 multigrain buns
4 slices red bell pepper
4 slices yellow bell pepper
½ red onion, thinly sliced
½ bunch watercress

- Preheat oven to 400°F (200°C).

- In a small bowl, mix together the garlic and oil and brush the tops and bottoms of mushrooms. In a baking dish, place mushrooms and season with salt and pepper. Bake for 30 minutes. The mushrooms will soften and some liquid with come out of them. Remove from oven and let cool.

- Top mushrooms with a portion of goat cheese and place under the broiler until the cheese begins to bubble.

- Spread mayonnaise on both sides of the bun and add a mushroom.

- Top with peppers, red onions, and watercress.

Makes 4 burgers.

MOROCCAN TURKEY BURGER

Christian and his brother Alain flew to Marrakesh, Morocco on Christmas Eve, 1972. They awoke the next morning to the sounds of the bustling market, or souk as it is called, which was next to their hotel. When they went to the market, they were amazed by the selection of foods available, as well as the stunning colors and aromas. Christian's memories of Marrakesh were the inspiration behind this Moroccan burger, which you can serve with lettuce and tomatoes and our Light Curry Mayonnaise (page 129).

½ cup onion, chopped
½ cup dried apricots
2 tbsp pine nuts
2 cloves garlic
1 ½ tsp cayenne powder
½ tsp cumin
½ tsp coriander
½ tsp salt
½ tsp freshly ground pepper
¼ tsp cinnamon
1 to 1 ½ lb ground turkey meat
2 tbsp olive oil
5 whole wheat sesame burger buns

- In a food processor, combine the onions, apricots, nuts, garlic, and all the spices and pulse until well blended.

- Transfer to a large mixing bowl, add turkey, and combine until mixture is well blended.

- Form into five 5-oz patties. (Do not make them too thin or they will fall apart.)

- Brush patties with oil and cook on a hot barbecue or grill about 6 minutes each side.

- Toast buns on grill, cut side down, for 1 to 2 minutes before patties are done.

Makes 5 burgers.

Brushing the patties with the oil keeps the moisture in the burgers.

Main Dishes

Potato-crusted Wild Pacific Salmon

Seared Wild Salmon
with Brown Butter, Lemon Capers
& Champagne Vinaigrette with Greens

Lemon Peppered Pacific Halibut

Bouillabaisse du Pacifique

Tomato-style Fish & Chips

Rigatoni with Chorizo

Free-range Chicken Breasts
in a Tarragon Mustard Marinade

Oven-roasted Lemon Rosemary Chicken

Grilled Beef Tenderloin

Best Ever Meatballs

Garlic Oregano Marinated Lamb Sirloin
with Almond Sage Pesto & Fig Jus

Chef's Baby Back Ribs with BBQ Sauce

Braised & Grilled Long Bone Pork Chops

Chef James's Butternut Squash Ravioli with
Brown Butter Sauce & Crispy Leeks

Christian's Basmati Fried Rice
with Marinated Tofu

Spinach & Swiss Chard Cannelloni

At the Tomato, Chef James Campbell's main dishes are inspired by fresh local seasonal products. This approach hearkens back to his roots in Atlantic Canada, where he eagerly awaited the changing of the seasons and the foods that each new season brought. A highlight each year was the opening of lobster season when families would gather on the beach for an annual lobster or corn boil. In the 1980s, when he moved to Toronto to pursue his culinary career, he found himself in the midst of a cooking revolution. It was a time of new, trendy restaurants, and young chefs using local and seasonal ingredients. James found it all very exciting, and dreamed of one day becoming a chef in a restaurant that shared the same philosophy and approach to food. Finding his way to the Tomato has, according to James (center photo below), "fulfilled my dream."

Check with your fishmonger to see what day of the week is best to buy fish, what freshwater items are available in season, and to make sure no product is endangered—be vigilant about sustainable practices. And no matter where you live, you can find farmer's markets that offer free-range and organic chickens, lamb, and beef, and an abundance of choice fruits and vegetables. Go to these markets and talk to the farmers themselves about their products and how they grow their crops and raise their animals. It's a great way to increase your awareness of environmental and agricultural issues—of knowing where your food comes from—and to support your local economy.

Highlights of this chapter include the Bouillabaisse du Pacifique (page 80), the Garlic Oregano Marinated Lamb Sirloin with Almond Sage Pesto & Fig Jus (page 88), and Chef James's Butternut Squash Ravioli with Brown Butter Sauce & Crispy Leeks (page 92).

POTATO-CRUSTED WILD PACIFIC SALMON

At the Tomato, we use local wild Pacific salmon; here on the west coast, the types of wild salmon available varies with the season. This dish is a real showstopper: the salmon is beautiful, and the crispy potato crust keeps the fish moist. We serve this with the Mediterranean Salsa (page 46) and simple organic salad greens topped with our Roasted Shallot Vinaigrette (page 123).

2 medium Yukon Gold or Russet potatoes, skins on
2 green onions, chopped
4 5-oz (140-g) salmon fillets
salt and freshly ground pepper to taste
2 tbsp canola oil
2 tbsp Dijon mustard

- Preheat oven to 425°F (240°C).

- In a large pot of boiling salted water, parboil the whole potatoes for about 10 minutes. (Parboiling means boiling until a knife inserted indicates they are still a bit firm inside.) Remove from heat and let cool completely (so they will be less starchy and won't stick together). Once cooled, remove skins from the potatoes. In a medium bowl, grate the potatoes, then combine with the green onions, season with salt and pepper, and set aside.

- Season the salmon with salt and pepper. In a large-ovenproof skillet on medium-high, heat the oil. Sear the salmon skin-side up for 2 minutes until browned.

- Remove salmon from the pan and brush the seared side of the salmon with the mustard. Spread ¼ cup of the potato and onion mixture on top of each fillet. (The mustard adds a nice flavor as well as adhering the potato to the fish.)

- Return the salmon back to the skillet, potato side down. Cook until the crust is golden brown. Flip the salmon over and place the pan into the oven for 3 to 4 minutes, or until the fish is slightly pink in the middle.

Makes 4 servings.

A fish spatula is a handy utensil to have. It's a heat-resistant, stainless steel spatula with slots in the blade, which is designed to support the weight of the fish. It has an offset handle to flip fish over easily.

When buying, fresh salmon should be firm to the touch and smell of the ocean but not fishy. Refrigerate salmon as soon as you arrive home, and use it the same day.

Seared Wild Salmon with Brown Butter, Lemon Capers & Champagne Vinaigrette with Greens

In this recipe, wild Pacific salmon is paired with fresh, seasonal greens from the market, keeping the focus on flavor, lightness, and simple presentation.

4 5-oz (125-g) wild salmon fillets
2 tbsp extra-virgin olive oil
¼ cup unsalted butter
juice of ½ lemon
2 tbsp capers, drained and rinsed
2 tbsp Italian parsley, chopped
2 medium shallots, finely minced
12 asparagus spears
1 tbsp olive oil (for asparagus)
salt and freshly ground pepper to taste
4 cups baby organic salad greens

Champagne Vinaigrette:

¼ cup champagne vinegar
1 tsp Dijon mustard
2 tbsp fresh parsley, chopped
2 shallots, minced
½ cup extra-virgin olive oil
salt and freshly ground pepper
   to taste

- Preheat the oven to 400°F (200°C).

- In a large, ovenproof skillet on high, heat the oil. Sear the salmon fillets 2 minutes per side. Transfer skillet to the oven and bake for 10 minutes for medium, or to preferred level of doneness.

- Remove from oven and place on a clean plate. Reserve any remaining juices in the pan, then return skillet to stove and add the butter on medium-high heat. When the butter begins to brown, add the lemon juice, capers, parsley, and shallots and sauté for 1 to 2 minutes. (Keep an eye on the butter so it doesn't burn.) Set aside.

- In a baking dish, lightly brush the asparagus with olive oil and season with salt and pepper. Roast for 4 to 5 minutes.

- While asparagus is roasting, in a small bowl combine the champagne vinegar, mustard, parsley, and shallots. Slowly whisk in the olive oil, then season with salt and pepper.

- To serve, combine the salad greens with the champagne vinaigrette and toss. Add the asparagus, then top with the salmon. Spoon brown butter over top.

Makes 4 servings.

LEMON PEPPERED PACIFIC HALIBUT

Chef James Campbell can cook fish so well he's been known to change the minds of a few of our regular customers who never liked fish before! Halibut is a mild, firm-textured fish that is as delicious as it is versatile. In this recipe, the halibut is seared in a skillet and then roasted in the oven. You can serve this dish with the Capellini Noodles tossed with Scallion Parsley Oil (page 119), the Summer-Roasted Roma Tomatoes (page 99), and the Roasted Baby Fennel Bulbs (page 106).

Crust:

zest of 5 lemons
1 tbsp coarse salt
1 tbsp coarse black pepper
1 tbsp fresh parsley, chopped

Fish:

4 5-oz (140-g) halibut fillets
2 tbsp canola oil
salt and freshly ground pepper to taste

- Preheat oven to 425°F (220°C).

- In a food processor or blender, combine the zest, salt, pepper, and parsley until well mixed. (You can make a larger quantity and store in the refrigerator for up to two weeks.)

- Spread about a 1 to 2 tsp of the lemon pepper mixture on each piece of halibut.

- In a large ovenproof skillet on medium-high, heat the oil. Sear the halibut–lemon pepper side first–for about 2 minutes, or until halibut starts to brown.

- Flip the halibut over and place pan in oven for 6 minutes, until the fish is firm but still moist inside.

Makes 4 servings.

Pacific halibut, which is caught as far north as Alaska, is milder in taste than Atlantic halibut. (Also, be aware that Atlantic halibut has been over-fished and some suggest avoiding it as the fishery tries to rebuild.) When buying halibut, look for fish that smells fresh like the ocean, and has firm white flesh. To store, rinse the fish under cold water and pat dry with paper towels, then keep refrigerated until ready to use.

BOUILLABAISSE DU PACIFIQUE

We always use seasonal local fish in our bouillabaisse: Salt Spring Island mussels, Savoury Island clams, local spot prawns, wild west coast salmon, Pacific halibut. Use whatever is fresh in your area. Serve this with the Saffron Rouille (page 139) on thinly-sliced toasted baguettes.

Broth:

¼ cup olive oil

½ tsp fennel seeds, crushed

2 cups leeks (white part only), washed and sliced

2 cups onions, sliced

3 cloves garlic, crushed

¼ cup tomato paste

2½ lbs (1 ¼ kg) halibut bones and 1 lb (500 g) salmon bones (excluding head), coarsely chopped

1 cup white wine

6 fresh Roma tomatoes or 1 14-oz (397-ml) can of whole plum tomatoes

2 tbsp each fresh thyme, parsley, basil, roughly chopped

½ tsp saffron

12 cups water

½ tsp each salt and pepper

Seafood Mixture:

6 small new potatoes, skins on, cooked to fork tender and halved

1 medium fennel bulb, julienned

6 large scallops

8 spotted prawns

12 clams, scrubbed

12 mussels, scrubbed and debearded

1 lb (500 g) mixed halibut and salmon, cut into 2-inch (5-cm) cubes

- In a large stockpot on medium, heat the oil then add the crushed fennel seeds. Sauté briefly (be careful not to burn), stirring until fragrant, approximately 30 seconds. Add the leeks, onions, and garlic and sauté until onions are softened, about 5 minutes.

- Stir in the tomato paste, coating the leek and onion mixture well. Brown lightly for 2 minutes. Rinse the fish bones then add to pot and brown for 5 minutes. Add the white wine and bring to a boil, then reduce heat and simmer for 5 minutes. Add the tomatoes, thyme, parsley, basil, saffron, and water. Bring to a full boil and then reduce to a roiling simmer. Cook for exactly 25 minutes.

- Using a mesh strainer, strain broth of bones, pushing to release all the juices. Skim excess oil from the top of the broth. Season with salt and pepper.

(Recipe continues on page 81)

Tomato Fresh Food Café Heirloom BLT Sandwich (page 66)

Portobello Burger (page 73)

Montreal Corned Beef Reuben Sandwich (page 72)

Heirloom tomatoes (page 36)

- Return the broth to stove and bring back to a boil. Reduce heat and simmer, then add the cooked potatoes, fennel, and all the seafood. Cover and simmer for 6 to 8 minutes. If any shellfish fail to open while cooking, discard them before serving.

Makes 4–6 servings (6 ½ cups in total).

For your bouillabaisse, choose approximately 5 to 6 oz (140 to 170 g) of both your favorite fish and shellfish, but stay away from leaner cuts of fish such as tuna as they tend to toughen up when boiled in a broth. Fish stock is traditionally made with white fish bones to give the stock a neutral flavor. Here we have used a modest amount of salmon bones, which makes this stock a bit richer.

TOMATO-STYLE FISH & CHIPS

Chef James Campbell makes this dish with a number of different fish: depending on what is fresh, available, and plentiful according to sustainable fishing guidelines (ling cod, Pacific halibut, and sole are good choices). Chef James's method, however, always stays the same. Serve it with the Tartar Sauce (page 131) and Pickled Cucumber and Sweet Pepper Salad (page 104).

Chips:

3 large Yukon Gold potatoes, skins on, cut
    into ¼-in (6-mm) slices or wedges
2–3 tbsp olive oil
salt and freshly ground pepper to taste

Fish:

1 cup all-purpose flour
salt and freshly ground pepper to taste
3 to 4 eggs, whisked

2 cups panko breadcrumbs
    (see note)
1 tbsp fresh parsley, chopped
zest of 2 lemons
4 to 6 pieces flat fish
    (see note above), 5 to 6 oz
    (140 to 170 g) per person
salt and freshly ground pepper
    (for fish)
2 cups canola oil for frying

- Preheat oven to 400°F (200°C).

- On a baking sheet, brush the potatoes with oil to coat. Season with salt and pepper and roast until tender and golded brown, about 20 minutes.

- While potatoes are roasting, set up a breading station for the fish, in this order: in one bowl, the flour seasoned with salt and pepper; in a second bowl, the whisked eggs; and in a third bowl, the panko crumbs, parsley, and lemon zest.

- Season the fish with salt and pepper, then coat with the flour, removing the excess. Next, coat with the eggs, then the panko seasoning mixture. Repeat until all the pieces of fish have been coated.

- In a frying pan on medium, heat just enough oil to fry two pieces of fish at a time. Carefully add the fish and cook until golden brown on both sides.

- Place fish in a baking dish and bake for 3 to 4 minutes to make sure fish is cooked through.

- Remove from oven and place on paper towels to soak up any excess oil.

- To serve, place 3 slices of potatoes on the plate and top with a piece of fish.

Makes 4–6 servings.

Panko breadcrumbs, Japanese in origin, can be found in Asian markets and now in many grocery stores. Panko yields a nice crispy crust when baked.

RIGATONI WITH CHORIZO

Chorizo is highly seasoned, coarsely ground pork sausage flavored with garlic, chili powder, and other spices. It's widely used in both Mexican and Spanish cookery; Mexican chorizo is made from fresh pork, while Spanish uses smoked pork. Chorizo is good in stews, soups, and eggs. Long-stemmed artichoke hearts come packed in oil in jars and can be found in most specialty or Italian markets and many gourmet grocers. They are fantastic, and can be grilled to give them additional flavor.

2 chorizo sausages
1 medium eggplant, sliced into ½-inch (2.5-cm) rounds
2 tbsp olive oil (for roasting eggplant)
salt and freshly ground pepper to taste
18 oz (500 g) dried rigatoni pasta, cooked
2 tbsp olive oil (to finish pasta)
2 tbsp olive oil (for sauté)
2 cloves garlic, minced
2 red bell peppers, roasted (see note)

2 yellow bell peppers, roasted (see note)
2 cups tomato sauce
6 long-stemmed artichoke hearts
⅓ cup fresh basil leaves, packed
2 oz (60 g) Parmigiana Reggiano cheese, grated
2 Roma tomatoes, oven-roasted (page 99) (optional)

- Preheat oven to 400°F (200°C).

- Place the chorizo sausages on a baking sheet. Pierce the sausage skins in several places and roast in oven until the skin is dark and crispy. Remove and let cool, then chop into chunks.

- In a blender or food processor, pulse sausage until ground.

- Reduce oven temperature to 350°F (180°C).

- On a baking sheet, toss the eggplant in the oil and season with salt and pepper. Bake for 20 minutes, or until eggplant is browned and soft. Let cool, then cut into 1-inch square cubes.

- While eggplant is roasting, in a pot of boiling salted water, cook the pasta for 5 to 7 minutes, until al dente. Drain, cool, and toss with oil to prevent noodles from sticking together.

- In a frying pan on medium-high, heat the oil. Sauté the garlic, ground chorizo, eggplant, roasted peppers, and tomato sauce for 2 minutes. Reduce heat, add the cooked pasta, and simmer to reduce any liquid. Stir in artichoke hearts. To serve, top with basil, cheese, and roasted tomatoes.

Makes 6 servings.

To roast the peppers, cut in half, remove seeds, brush with oil, and roast in oven at 350°F (180°C) for 10 minutes. Cut into 1-inch cubes.

FREE-RANGE CHICKEN BREASTS IN A TARRAGON MUSTARD MARINADE

Our free-range chickens come from the Fraser Valley in British Columbia, but free-range varieties are now available everywhere. They are known for their superior flavor and tenderness; they are raised on natural diets, and are allowed plenty of room to roam about. Serve this with the Roasted Sieglinde Potatoes (page 111).

Marinade:

¼ cup Dijon mustard
2 shallots, minced
½ jalapeño pepper, seeded and minced
6 tbsp fresh tarragon, chopped (see note)
2 tbsp soy sauce
½ tsp black pepper
¾ cup olive oil

Chicken:

4 free-range chicken breasts,
   bone in (7–8 oz/200–225 g
   each)
3 tbsp vegetable oil
1 cup chicken stock

- In a blender or food processor, combine all the marinade ingredients except the oil and blend for 1 minute. Slowly add the oil while continuing to blend. Place the chicken breasts in a large dish, and cover with marinade. Marinate, covered, in the refrigerator for at least 1 hour.

- Preheat oven to 425°F (220°C).

- In a large ovenproof frying pan on high, heat the oil. Sear the chicken breasts skin-side down for about 1 minute, until golden brown. Flip over and brown the other side.

- Add the chicken stock and roast in oven for 15 to 20 minutes. (This quick-braising method means that the chicken will always be tender.) Check at the wishbone to ensure there is no blood; alternatively, an instant read thermometer should read 170°F (75°C).

- When the chicken breasts are done, remove them from the pan and reduce the pan juices on the stove until thickened.

- Serve chicken with the pan jus.

Makes 4 servings.

Tarragon is an herb frequently used in French cooking to flavor vegetables like young carrots, peas, and beets, and with eggs, chicken, delicate fish like halibut, and other seafood. Tarragon has a peppery, anise-like flavor that goes well with lemon and Dijon mustard.

The marinade by itself will keep in the refrigerator for up to 7 to 10 days.

OVEN-ROASTED LEMON ROSEMARY CHICKEN

Lemon and rosemary infuse this chicken with fresh, bold flavors, and the combination of sherry and whipping cream makes a rich sauce. Leftovers can be used to make the Oven-Roasted Lemon Rosemary Chicken Sandwich (page 69).

Chicken:

1 3-lb whole free-range chicken
salt and pepper to taste
1 lemon, sliced into quarters
1 onion, sliced into quarters

Sauce:

1 ounce sherry or port
¼ cup whipping cream, 33% milkfat

Paste:

3 tbsp grainy Dijon mustard
2 tbsp olive oil
1 tbsp chili powder
2 cloves garlic, finely chopped
1 tbsp sherry vinegar
2 to 3 tbsp fresh rosemary leaves, finely chopped

- Preheat oven to 375°F (190°C).

- Remove the neck from chicken cavity, then rinse and dry the chicken. Salt and pepper the cavity, then stuff with the lemon and onion slices.

- In a small bowl, combine together all the ingredients for the paste. Generously coat the outside of the chicken as well as under the skin of the breast (you can gently separate the skin from the flesh with your fingers). If desired, refrigerate for ½ to 1 hour to enhance the flavor.

- Truss chicken and place in a roasting pan. Roast for 25 minutes per pound, until juices run clear.

- Remove chicken from the pan and cover with foil to keep it warm. Allow to rest for 10 minutes before serving.

- While chicken rests, heat the pan juices on top of the stove. Add sherry or port and bring to a boil, then reduce heat and add the whipping cream.

- Simmer for 2–3 minutes, scraping pan bottom with a wooden spoon to remove pan drippings.

- Drizzle over the chicken before serving.

Makes 4 servings.

"Fryers" and "Boilers" are the most common chickens for oven roasting and barbequing. They are young chickens, 7 to 13 weeks old, and weigh from 2 ½ to 5 lbs (1 to 2.5 kg). Choose chicken with plump breasts that are odorless, and have no tears in the skin. Whole chickens and chicken pieces are properly cooked when the breast registers 160°F to 165° F (70°C to 75°C) and the thigh registers 165°F to 175°F (75°C to 80°C).

If you can, use organic chicken whenever possible. Chicken certified as organic have been raised on organic feed free of medications and additives, and have access to sunlight and space to move about.

GRILLED BEEF TENDERLOIN

This superb dish is easy to prepare and extremely tender, with intense flavor. We serve it with the Chipotle Butter (page 138) and the Buttermilk Mashed Potatoes (page 112).

4 5-oz (140-g) beef tenderloin steaks
2 to 3 tbsp olive oil
salt and freshly ground pepper to taste

- Rub the steaks with oil, and season with salt and pepper on both sides.

- Heat a grill (see note). Alternatively, place a heavy frying pan on medium-high heat. When pan is very hot, add the steaks to sear.

- Grill for 4 to 5 minutes per side for medium rare, depending on thickness. For medium, 8 minutes per side; for medium-well, 10 minutes per side.

Makes 4 servings.

The Tomato gets its beef from Ranchland Natural Foods from the Cutter Ranch in the Nicola Valley near Merritt, BC. They sell free-range beef that is hormone and antibiotic-free, with a 21-day aging process that enhances both flavor and tenderness. We do these steaks on a grill, but you can also use a heavy frying pan. Tenderloin is the most tender cut you can buy, has the least fat among all cuts of beef, and is the most expensive. It is, however, quick and easy to prepare.

BEST EVER MEATBALLS

These meatballs with the Quick Weekday Tomato Sauce (page 134) make a great combination on top of your favorite pasta; they're also good with our Buttermilk Mashed Potatoes (page 112). Christian and I call this combination comfort food, the kinds of meals we make at home when we want to chase away the "winter blues"; here, in Vancouver, that means a rainy day. These meatballs also can be made ahead of time and frozen for that "rainy day."

1 lb (500 g) lean ground beef
1 cup breadcrumbs
1 large egg
1 small onion, finely chopped
2 tsp Madras curry powder
2 tbsp Dijon mustard
2 tsp chili powder
1 tsp salt
1 tsp freshly ground pepper
½ jalapeño pepper, seeded and finely chopped
1 clove garlic, chopped
1½ cups panko breadcrumbs
2 tbsp olive oil

- Preheat oven to 350°F (180°C).
- In a large bowl, combine all the ingredients except the panko breadcrumbs and olive oil.
- Form the mixture into 20 golf ball-sized meatballs, then roll in breadcrumbs, and place on a baking sheet lined with foil. Drizzle oil over top of the meatballs.
- Bake for 20 minutes.

Makes 4 servings.

Panko breadcrumbs, Japanese in origin, can be found in Asian markets and now in many grocery stores. Panko yields a nice crispy crust when baked.

For a variation, make a meat loaf with the same ingredients. Combine everything but panko breadcrumbs and oil and shape into a 9 × 5-inch (23 × 13-cm) loaf pan. Brush with the oil and sprinkle panko crumbs on top. Bake in a 350°F (180°C) oven for 1 ¼ hours. Makes 4 servings.

Garlic Oregano Marinated Lamb Sirloin with Almond Sage Pesto & Fig Jus

For a special occasion or if you want to impress dinner guests, try making these lamb sirloins. They are particularly flavorful and tender with the almond sage pesto and sweet fig port sauce. A simple dish to prepare, and a favorite on our dinner menu, we serve it with the Butternut Squash & Yukon Gold Potato Gratin (page 116).

4 5- to 7-oz (140- to 200-g) lamb sirloins

Marinade (makes 1 cup):

4 to 6 cloves garlic
½ cup loosely packed fresh oregano leaves
2 tbsp sherry vinegar
2 tbsp freshly squeezed lemon juice
2 tbsp freshly squeezed lime juice
2 tbsp honey
2 tsp ancho chili powder
¼ tsp salt
1 cup olive oil

Almond Sage Pesto (makes 1 cup):

2 cups fresh parsley, loosely packed
1 cup almonds, sliced
½ cup Parmesan cheese, grated
⅓ cup fresh sage leaves
2 cloves garlic
½ tsp salt
¾ cup olive oil

Fig Jus (makes ⅔ cup):

1 tbsp olive oil
6 mission figs, fresh or dried, diced
1 shallot, minced
½ cup port or cranberry juice
1 cup good quality demi-glace
salt to taste

For the marinade:

- In a blender or food processor, blend all the marinade ingredients except the oil. While continuing to blend, slowly add the oil until the marinade looks like a creamy dressing.

- In a shallow pan, place the lamb sirloins and add enough marinade to coat.

- Cover and let marinate in the refrigerator for at least 1 hour.

For the pesto:

- In a blender or food processor, blend all the ingredients except the oil until finely chopped. While continuing to blend, slowly add the oil until consistency is thick enough to hold its own shape. (This consistency allows the pesto to "stick" to the sirloin without melting off.)

For the lamb:

- Preheat oven to 400°F (200°C).

- In an ovenproof skillet on medium-high, heat 1 tbsp oil. Sear the lamb sirloins until golden brown on both sides, about 2 to 3 minutes. Remove and coat one side of each loin with 2 tbsp pesto.

- Roast for 12 minutes for medium rare, 16 minutes for medium, and 18 minutes for well done. Let meat rest for 4 to 5 minutes before cutting into ¼-inch (6-mm) slices.

For the fig jus:

- In a frying pan on medium-high, heat the oil. Sauté the figs and shallot for 2 minutes. Deglaze pan with the port, add the demi-glace, and reduce on high heat for 4 minutes. Add salt to taste.

Makes 4–6 servings.

 The sirloin comes from the hip of lamb and is the leanest cut on the animal. In Australia, it is called the chump.

CHEF'S BABY BACK RIBS WITH BBQ SAUCE

This is a wonderful dish to share with friends that can be prepared at any time of the year. Just change what you serve with the ribs according to the season. Make extra and have some the next day!

4 1-lb (500-g) Danish baby back ribs
2 tsp cumin
2 tsp salt
2 tsp freshly ground pepper
¼ cup vegetable oil
6 carrots, peeled and chopped into 1-in (2.5-cm) pieces
6 stalks celery, chopped into 1-in (2.5-cm) pieces
2 onions, cut into quarters

¼ cup tomato paste
6 cups chicken stock
BBQ Sauce (page 133)

Bouquet garni (see note):

1 tbsp whole black peppercorns
3 bay leaves
⅛ cup fresh thyme

- Preheat oven to 350°F (180°C).

- Season the ribs with the cumin, salt, and pepper. In a large roasting pan on medium-high heat, brown the ribs in the oil on both sides. Remove from pan.

- Add the carrots, celery, and onions, and sauté until they start to softened. Add the tomato paste and cook for another 5 minutes.

- Add the chicken stock and bring to a boil, then remove from heat. Return the ribs to the pan; add the bouquet garni.

- Cover with foil and roast for 90 minutes.

- Remove ribs from roasting pan and brush both sides with BBQ Sauce then place on a baking sheet and roast for another 20 minutes.

Makes 4 servings.

Baby back ribs come from the pig's loin section; these ribs are smaller and more rounded than side ribs. Back ribs are more tender and have a greater meat-to-the-bone ratio than side ribs. Danish back ribs are our choice for this recipe. When purchasing, try to find slabs that are 2 lb (I kg) or less.

A bouquet garni is made by tying fresh herbs with kitchen string, or placing them in a cheesecloth bag secured with a string to make them easy to remove before serving. The classic bouquet garni combines parsley, thyme, and bay leaf.

BRAISED & GRILLED LONG BONE
PORK CHOPS

Pork loin is a very lean cut of meat, and braising the entire loin rack to medium-rare, then cutting it into chops for grilling or barbecuing, helps to build better flavor. If you don't have or don't want to use a barbecue, you can finish cooking the pork rack in the oven. This is a rich, comforting fall dish best served with Buttermilk Mashed Potatoes (page 112) and Pear Chutney (page 140).

1 6-rib rack or Frenched prime pork roast, fat cap removed (approx. 2.5 lbs or 1 kg)
1 tsp salt
1 tsp freshly ground pepper
3 tbsp canola oil
3 medium carrots, peeled and roughly chopped
1 onion, roughly chopped
3 stalks celery, roughly chopped
¼ cup tomato paste
1 cup dry white wine
3 cups chicken stock

- Preheat oven to 325°F (160°C).

- Season the pork with salt and pepper.

- In a large roasting pan on medium-high, heat the oil. Sear the pork on all sides, about 5 minutes. Remove from the pan and set aside.

- Reduce heat to medium and stir in the carrots, onions, and celery. Sauté until softened, about 10 to 12 minutes. Add the tomato paste and mix well. Sauté for another 3 to 5 minutes, then add the wine and chicken stock. Increase heat and bring to a boil.

- Remove pan from heat and return the pork rack. Cover with foil and braise in oven for 70 minutes, or until the meat registers 160°F (70°C) on a meat thermometer.

- When done, remove pork rack from braising liquid. Let stand, loosely covered with foil, to rest for 10 minutes before cutting into individual chops. Strain liquid through a fine mesh strainer and reduce further to make a sauce.

- Optional last step: barbecue the pork by removing the rack from the oven 10 minutes earlier. After resting, cut into chops and complete cooking on the barbecue or grill for 10 minutes.

Makers 4–6 servings.

Today, pork is 47% leaner than ten years ago. When buying pork, look for pale pink meat with white, not yellow, fat, an indication of a younger, more tender cut of meat.

CHEF JAMES'S BUTTERNUT SQUASH RAVIOLI WITH BROWN BUTTER SAUCE & CRISPY LEEKS

Chef James developed this recipe for New Year's Eve—it's the type of dish meant for a special occasion. The pasta is not difficult to make, but it requires a pasta machine and takes some planning because the dough needs to chill for one hour before using.

Dough:

- 6 large egg yolks
- 1 large egg
- 1½ tsp olive oil
- 1 tbsp milk
- 1¾ cups all-purpose flour

Brown butter sauce:

- ½ cup unsalted butter

Crispy leeks:

- 2 cups vegetable oil
- 1 leek (white part only), julienned
- salt to taste

Filling:

- 1 large butternut squash, halved and seeded (1½ lbs or 680 g)
- 2 tbsp mascarpone cheese
- ⅛ tsp cinnamon
- ⅛ tsp ground nutmeg
- ⅛ tsp cloves
- ⅛ tsp ground ginger
- salt and pepper to taste

For the dough:

- In a large bowl, mix together the egg yolks, whole egg, oil, and milk. In a separate bowl, add the flour, making a well in center, then gradually stir in the egg mixture with a spatula, pulling the flour in until incorporated (the dough should be moist but not sticky).

- Place dough on a lightly floured surface and knead until it feels silky smooth. Wrap dough in plastic and refrigerate for at least 1 hour, up to overnight.

For the filling:

- Preheat oven to 400°F (200°C).

- On a baking sheet, cut side down, bake squash for 45 to 55 minutes, or until tender. Let cool and then scoop out the flesh. In a large bowl, combine the squash with the mascarpone, spices, salt, and pepper and mix well.

For the pasta:

- Remove the dough from the refrigerator and bring to room temperature before using. Divide it into 3 pieces and flatten just enough to fit through a pasta machine. Put dough through machine one notch at a time, until the thinnest setting is reached, resulting in long sheets of pasta.

- On a lightly-floured surface, lay one sheet of the pasta down and place 1 tbsp filling at a time, 2 inches (5 cm) apart. Lay another sheet of pasta on top removing any air between the two sheets of pasta. Seal the all edges with water, then cut into 3 ½ by 3 ½-inch squares. Repeat until dough and filling are used up.

- In a large pot of boiling salted water, cook the ravioli for 3 minutes. They will float to the top when they are done. Drain and set aside.

For the brown butter sauce:

- In a saucepan on medium, heat the butter until it turns golden brown but not burnt. Drizzle on top of pasta just before serving.

For the crispy leeks:

- In a deep-sided pot, heat the oil to 375°F (190°C). Deep-fry julienned leeks; they will float to the top of the oil when done. Place on paper towels to drain, season with salt, and place on top of pasta.

Makes 4 servings.

A winter squash, butternut is similar in shape to a large pear and is sweetest when no bigger than 12 inches long and 5 inches in diameter. In fact, the smaller the butternut, the sweeter the flavor.

CHRISTIAN'S BASMATI FRIED RICE WITH MARINATED TOFU

On his travels through South India, Christian ended up in Pondicherry, a seaside town that has a French colonial heritage. While there, he worked in the private home of Mr. Utar, a biologist from Holland who was doing research on butterflies. Christian worked as Mr. Utar's personal chef, making his meals and going to the market on his bicycle every day to buy fish, vegetables, and exotic fruits. During his stay, he learned a very simple way to cook rice, which is similar to that for cooking pasta. This dish was inspired by Christian's time in India.

Marinated Tofu:

½ pkg (6 oz or 175 g) extra-firm tofu, cubed into 1-inch pieces

1 tbsp olive oil

1 tsp balsamic vinegar

1 tsp smoked paprika or Madras curry powder

1 tsp sea salt

1 tbsp olive oil (for sauté)

Fried Rice:

1 cup uncooked basmati brown rice

1 tsp salt

3 medium carrots, diced

1 cup broccoli, chopped into 1-inch pieces

2 to 3 tbsp olive oil

1 small onion, diced

1 small zucchini, diced

½ cup mushrooms, sliced

½ cup red bell pepper, diced

2 cloves garlic, chopped

1 tsp fresh ginger, grated

3 tbsp Madras curry powder

1 tsp salt

½ tsp freshly ground pepper

1 tsp chili flakes

1 tsp oil (for eggs)

2 large eggs

pinch of salt and pepper

¼ cup fresh cilantro leaves, chopped

For the tofu:

- In a medium bowl, marinate the tofu in the oil, vinegar, curry powder, and salt for 10 to 15 minutes. In a frying pan on medium heat, sauté the marinated tofu in the oil until just warm. Set aside.

For the rice:

- Rinse the rice several times in cold water. In a medium pot, cover the rice with cold water. Add the salt and bring to a boil, uncovered. Reduce heat to medium, and cook for approximately 40 to 45 minutes. Rice should be still tender but not soft. Add water during cooking, if necessary.

- When the rice is done, strain. Return rice to the pot, cover, and let sit for 10 minutes.

- While rice rests, in a pot of boiling salted water, cook the carrots and broccoli and cook for 5 to 6 minutes until they start to soften.

- In a frying pan or wok on medium, heat the oil. Sauté the onions, zucchini, mushrooms, peppers, garlic, ginger, curry powder, salt, pepper, chili flakes, and marinated tofu for about 5 minutes. Stir in the cooked carrots and broccoli and sauté for an additional 3 minutes. Add the cooked rice and stir through.
- In a skillet on medium, heat the 1 tsp oil. Add the eggs and scramble for 2 minutes until cooked. Add a pinch of salt and pepper. Roughly chop the eggs, then add eggs and cilantro to the fried rice and mix well.

Makes 4 servings.

SPINACH & SWISS CHARD CANNELLONI

Swiss chard (or just plain chard) is known for its edible stalks and leaves rich in vitamins and minerals. Choose chard that is firm and unblemished with crisp, evenly-colored leaves. It can be eaten raw or cooked; when small and tender, the raw leaves are delicious in salads. In cooked dishes, chard leaves are prepared much like spinach. This recipe uses unique yet simple ingredients to create an irresistible, sumptuous dish.

2 bunches ruby red Swiss chard
    (about 12 large leaves)
4 cups spinach
2 tbsp olive oil
1 small onion, diced
4 to 6 cloves garlic
1 15 oz (475 g) container ricotta cheese
1 cup fresh mozzarella cheese, grated
½ cup fresh Parmesan cheese, grated
¼ cup fresh basil leaves, roughly chopped

pinch of ground nutmeg
pinch of salt and freshly ground
    pepper
3 fresh 9 ×12-inch pasta sheets or
    dried equivalent, cooked
2 cups Quick Weekday Tomato
    Sauce (page 134)
1 cup fresh mozzarella cheese,
    grated (to sprinkle on top)

- Preheat oven to 375°F (190°C).

- Wash the chard and spinach carefully to remove sand, then roughly chop and set aside.

- In a skillet on medium, heat the oil. Sauté the onions until softened. Add the garlic and sauté for an additional 3 minutes.

- Add the spinach and chard, reduce heat to low, and sauté until the greens become wilted and the liquid evaporates, about 7 minutes. Set aside to cool.

- In a large mixing bowl, combine the three cheeses, basil, nutmeg, salt, and pepper. Add the cooked spinach and chard and mix well.

- Place mixture into a tipless piping bag or a zip-lock plastic bag with one corner cut off. Lay out the pasta sheets on the counter and pipe a line of the mixture along the two longest outside edges of each sheet.

- Roll each side toward the middle. Cut in half lengthwise and then cut each tube in half so each sheet produces four evenly-rolled tubes. Repeat until all the mixture has been used.

- Grease a 14 × 9 × 2-inch (33 × 23 × 5-cm) baking dish. Place a thin layer of tomato sauce in bottom of the dish. Arrange cannelloni, seam sides down, in the sauce. Ladle remaining sauce over top and sprinkle with grated mozzarella. Bake, uncovered, for 25 to 30 minutes, or until warmed through and the cheese has melted and tomato sauce starts to bubble.

Makes 6 servings.

Cannelloni freeze well for up to 4 to 6 weeks.

Fresh pasta sheets can be purchased at pasta specialty shops and grocery stores in the refrigerated section.

Grilled Beef Tenderloin (page 86) with Buttermilk Mashed Potatoes (page 112)

Free-Range Chicken Breasts in a Tarragon Mustard Marinade (page 84)

Sautéed Prawns with Fresh Ginger Orange
Lime Sauce & Sesame Oil Soba Noodles (page 52)

Potato-crusted Wild Pacific Salmon (page 77)

Vegetables and Side Dishes

Summer-Roasted Roma Tomatoes

Oven-Roasted Asparagus with Pine Nuts &
Shaved Parmesan Cheese

Scarlet Runner Beans with Dry-Cured
Hungarian Salami

Pickled Cucumber & Sweet Pepper Salad

Roasted Bell Peppers

Roasted Baby Fennel Bulbs

Broccolini with Crispy Garlic & Fermented
Black Beans

BBQ Peaches & Cream Corn on the Cob

Roasted Root Vegetables

Baby Organic Carrots with Ginger, Chives & Mint

Roasted Sieglinde Potatoes

Buttermilk Mashed Potatoes

Cauliflower, Corn & Toasted Almond Succotash

Brussels Sprouts
with Chili Orange Maple Butter

Butternut Squash & Yukon Gold Potato Gratin

Parmesan Ricotta Polenta

Wild Mushroom Risotto

Capellini Noodles Tossed in Scallion Parsley Oil

Corn Relish

My mom Carell was a vegetarian who thrived on grains, beans, and a huge variety of vegetables. My father Andy, on the other hand, ate mostly meat (steak), vine-ripened tomatoes, and roasted potatoes. Mom cooked for the family as if she were a restaurant chef, having to cater to everyone's various tastes. She taught me a lot about food; we spent countless hours finding ingredients to make lentil patties, the right beans for a three-bean salad, or unique vegetables like kuri squash or kohlrabi, which tastes like a mild turnip. We even grew our own alfalfa and sunflower sprouts. My father was involved too; he taught me the value of shopping every day for the evening's meal. He would pick up vegetables as well as stop at the local butcher shop on his way home as a part of his daily routine.

Meal preparation and eating were true adventures in my family's home. Yet at the time, I thought our neighbors who only bought their groceries once a week were pretty smart. Why bother to shop for food every day? I didn't understand the importance of obtaining the freshest ingredients available, and only when you needed them. But what a legacy my parents left me: a desire to seek out the best places to buy fresh, local, and in season.

You'll find lots of great vegetable recipes in this chapter, some of which I hope will become your favorites. Oven-Roasted Asparagus with Pine Nuts & Shaved Parmesan Cheese (page 101) is a great dish for spring, when asparagus is young and tender. A summer favorite, which uses baby broccoli and fresh garlic from the garden, is the Broccolini with Crispy Garlic & Fermented Black Beans (page 107). For fall, try the Wild Mushroom Risotto (page 118). And the Butternut Squash & Yukon Gold Potato Gratin (page 116) is a perennial favorite in winter, when we all crave traditional comfort foods.

Summer-Roasted Roma Tomatoes

In August and September, when Roma tomatoes are ripe, pick them straight off the vine and roast them. Roasting caramelizes the sugar and intensifies the flavors. They're also versatile: you can add roasted tomatoes to a platter of antipasto, on top of pastas and salads, or in sandwiches, soups, and frittatas. They go well with a variety of herbs; see the list on the following page for some of our favorite "tomato" herbs.

2 lbs (1 kg) Roma tomatoes, quartered
¼ cup olive oil
2 tbsp balsamic vinegar
2 cloves garlic, minced
2 tsp fresh oregano, chopped
¼ tsp salt
⅛ tsp freshly ground pepper

- Preheat oven to 350°F (180°C).

- In a large bowl, toss all the ingredients together and mix well.

- Bake on a foil-lined tray until tomatoes are sugary and caramelized, 1 ¼ to 1 ½ hours.

Makes 4 servings.

Herbs & Tomatoes

Summer-roasted tomatoes go well with a variety of herbs: oregano, basil, thyme, chives, even rosemary. Try any of these as variations.

Oregano is a Greek herb that belongs to the mint family. It has a strong, pungent aroma and a peppery bite. Oregano goes well with all tomato-based dishes, as well as roasted potatoes, eggplant, lamb, and squid.

Basil is another Mediterranean herb belonging to the mint family. Fresh basil's flavor is a spicy mix of anise and cloves. There are several varieties of basil with green leaves, as well as opal basil, which has deep purple leaves; vinegar infused with opal basil actually takes on the purple color. Basil is an essential ingredient in Italian pesto and goes well with tomatoes, salads, sauces, dressings, meats, and fish. It's also good as a topping for pizza (the simple Margherita) or to accompany fresh mozzarella. Basil loses flavor when cooked so it is best added near the end of the cooking process.

Thyme is a basic herb in French cuisine. It is also part of the mint family and is native to southern Europe and the Mediterranean. Thyme has a robust flavor and spicy fragrance. Use it in stews and soups, and with eggs, beans, lentils, meats, and all seafood. Thyme also goes well with many fruits, in particular figs and pears.

Chives are related to the leek and onion but have a milder flavor. They complement dishes that use eggs, cheese, vegetables, and chicken. Their lavender flowers are edible and great used in salads.

Rosemary is very aromatic and grows wild in the Mediterranean. It's a woody evergreen shrub with needle-shaped leaves having the flavor of sweet pine with hints of lemon. Rosemary is great when grilling meats, with poultry, or seafood such as shrimp, mussels, and tuna. Try using it finely chopped and sprinkled on top of foccacia and in small amounts with apples and pears.

OVEN-ROASTED ASPARAGUS WITH PINE NUTS & SHAVED PARMESAN CHEESE

Locally grown asparagus can be found in many places around North America, but in abundance only in spring when the spears are young, tender, and fleshy. Whether the spears are thin or thick, you need to trim the stem ends, which can be tough, by snapping off the last 1 ½ inches. This recipe oven roasts them, but in summer, you can fire up the barbecue and grill them.

1 lb (500 g) asparagus, ends trimmed
1 to 2 tbsp olive oil
salt and freshly ground pepper
¼ cup pine nuts, toasted (see note)
¼ cup or 2 oz shaved Parmesan cheese

- Preheat oven to 350°F (180°C).

- On a baking tray, arrange asparagus, drizzle with olive oil, and season with salt and pepper. Bake for 15 to 20 minutes, or until tender.

- Remove from oven. Place asparagus on a platter and sprinkle with the toasted pine nuts.

- Using a potato peeler, shave pieces of Parmesan cheese on top.

Makes 4 servings.

There are over 300 varieties of asparagus. Fresh asparagus should be free of "rust," and the heads should never show signs of "flowering." If buying a large quantity, select similarly-sized bunches so that they will cook evenly. Wash spears well in cold water to get rid of soil and sand. Properly-cooked asparagus should be bright green and slightly firm when poked with a fork; overcooking will make it pale and lose flavor. Most asparagus is green, but you can buy purple and white varieties (the latter of which is simply green asparagus grown in the dark). It's a highly perishable vegetable, but will keep for up to 3 days in the refrigerator wrapped in a damp cloth or placed in a perforated plastic bag.

Pine nuts, also are known as pinon or pignoli, are tiny cream-colored nuts that are high in protein. They come from pine trees, specifically from inside pine cones, which have to be heated to remove the nuts. This process is very labor-intensive, which makes these nuts more expensive than most. Purchase small quantities because they can quickly go rancid due to their high fat content. They can be stored airtight in the refrigerator for up to 3 months or frozen for 9 months. Pine nuts are a key ingredient in classic Italian pesto.

To roast pine nuts: Place nuts on a baking tray in a 350°F (180°C) oven for 8 to 10 minutes, until golden brown.

Susan's Glorious Greens

At the Tomato Fresh Food Café, we buy our organic greens from Susan Davidson of Glorious Garnish and Seasonal Salad Company in Aldergrove, BC. Glorious Garnish evolved from a 1985 Employment Opportunity grant, whose mandate was to research ways to supplement livelihoods on small parcels of land. They chose to develop a business supplying pre-cut, ready-to-eat salads to Vancouver's restaurants, something no other grower was doing at the time.

Today, the Tomato orders more greens from Glorious Garnish than any other restaurant in the city. Twice a week for about eight months of the year, Susan delivers right to our door. We receive as much as 800 pounds (350 kilos) of leafy greens per month! For two years running, Susan has presented Christian with a crown and a certificate that named him "King of the Greens."

If Christian is the "king" of greens, then Parminder Deol and Harjinder Deol, employees of Glorious Garnish, are the "queens." Parminder and Harjinder, along with Manjit and Auntie (see photo below), put a lot of tender loving care into the salad greens that make up the "Celebration" mix, a blend of 25 to 30 herbs, wild and cultivated greens, and edible flowers. The Sikhs are the backbone of the agriculture industry in British Columbia's Fraser Valley, arriving in the area about 1910 from the Punjab area of India, where they have farmed for decades. They are strong, hard-working people whose spiritual faith embraces a reverence for the land and the food they grow. Using kitchen scissors, "the Inders" hand-clip the greens, and then clean and dry them in a large centrifuging salad spinner. Over the years, they have taken on more and more "ownership" of the salad, adding the tips of chickpea plants and methi greens from Sikh cuisine. Of course, the mixture also changes with the seasons. In the summer, the mixture might include everything from pea shoots to marigold flowers and rose petals, while in the fall it might contain spinach and kale.

Susan and Glorious Garnish also supply the Tomato with many other vegetables, including gold, white, and striped baby beets; red, white, purple, and yellow carrots; leeks; Russet and Belle de Boskoop apples (see recipe, page 174); kuri squash; Stringless Scarlet Runner Beans (see recipe, page 103); edamame; fava beans; collard tips; watercress; Swiss chard; spinach; arugula; and strawberry rhubarb.

Susan and her glorious greens can be found every Saturday from the middle of May to October at the Trout Lake Farmers' Market in East Vancouver. She's the kind of caring, hands-on organic farmer you will want to find near you.

SCARLET RUNNER BEANS WITH DRY-CURED HUNGARIAN SALAMI

Scarlet runner beans are sweet-tasting white beans from fast-growing vines with an abundance of attractive scarlet flowers in showy clusters. The beans are thick, flat, 6- to 8-inches long, and are available from mid-summer to September, or until the nights get cold. The bean pods are delicious when young. When mature, shell the beans and cook them as you would lima beans.

1 lb (500 g) scarlet runner or other broad beans
1 tbsp olive oil
1 large clove garlic, finely chopped
¼ cup dry-cured Hungarian salami, finely chopped
salt and freshly ground pepper to taste

- In a pot of boiling salted water, blanch the beans by boiling them for five minutes and then immediately immersing them in ice water to stop the cooking process. Remove beans from water soon as they are cool. Set aside.

- In a frying pan, sauté the garlic and salami in oil for 2 minutes. Add the beans and sauté for an additional 2 minutes. Season with salt and pepper.

Makes 4 servings.

This recipe can also be used with green beans or with the small French haricots verts; just watch the cooking time, as the smaller the beans, the less time they take to cook. Haricots verts are a refined variety of the domestic green bean; they are long and slim, with a delicate, sweet flavor. They contain fewer seeds and less water than other string beans.

PICKLED CUCUMBER & SWEET PEPPER SALAD

This Asian-inspired dish is not so much a salad as it is a garnish or condiment that we serve in place of a sauce with halibut, prawns, and our Tomato-Style Fish & Chips (page 82).

1 long English cucumber, seeded, cut in half and julienned
½ red bell pepper, julienned
½ yellow bell pepper, julienned
¼ red onion, julienned
¼ cup rice vinegar (see note)
¼ cup mirin (see note)

- In a small bowl, combine all the ingredients and toss well.

- Covered or in a sealed container, this salad will keep in the refrigerator for 2 to 3 days.

Makes 2 cups.

Rice vinegar is made from fermented rice and is milder than most Western vinegars. Japanese rice vinegar is used in sushi rice. Mirin is a sweet, rice wine that is golden in color and has a low alcohol content. It is made from glutinous rice and considered essential to Japanese cooking.

ROASTED BELL PEPPERS

From mid-summer to fall, farmer's markets are abundant with all kinds of peppers. Best known are the mild bell peppers, which come in various sizes, shapes, and colors—green, red, yellow, orange, and purple. There's also an extraordinary variety of chili peppers available, with heat ranging from mild to hot to flaming. All peppers can be roasted. When buying them, look for smooth, shiny unblemished skin.

4 bell peppers any variety, seeded, cored, and cut in half
2 tbsp olive oil
salt and freshly ground pepper to taste

- Preheat the oven to 400°F (200°C).

- In a large bowl, toss the peppers in the oil. Place skin-sides up on a baking sheet and roast for 30 to 35 minutes.

- Place roasted peppers back into bowl, cover with plastic wrap, and allow to steam for 10 minutes, or until the skins loosen and are easy to remove.

- These will keep in the refrigerator for 1 week.

Makes 4 servings.

ROASTED BABY FENNEL BULBS

Fennel has a strong anise flavor that complements fish, pastas, soups, and bouillabaisse. The bulbs can be thinly sliced and served raw in salads and coleslaw. When buying, choose firm, bulbs with no bruising. We especially like the small baby fennel, but if using larger fennel bulbs, remove the outermost leaves.

4 baby fennel bulbs, chopped into quarters
¼ tsp salt
¼ tsp freshly ground pepper
1 tbsp olive oil

- Preheat oven to 400°F (200°C).

- In a bowl, toss the fennel with the salt, pepper, and oil.

- Place on a baking tray and roast for 30 to 35 minutes, until tender.

Makes 4 servings.

BROCCOLINI WITH CRISPY GARLIC & FERMENTED BLACK BEANS

Broccolini has smaller florets that are sweeter and more tender than those of its broccoli cousin. We toss broccolini with crispy garlic and fermented black beans found in Asian markets, which should be soaked in water to remove any of the excess salt in which they are preserved. The toasted sesame oil adds great flavor to this dish.

½ lb (250 g) broccolini, stems trimmed by ¼ inch
2 cloves garlic, thinly sliced
1 tbsp olive oil
3 tbsp fermented black beans
1 tsp toasted sesame oil
salt and freshly ground pepper to taste

- In a pot of boiling salted water, cook the broccolini for 7 minutes, or until tender enough to poke with a fork. Strain and set aside.

- In a large frying pan on medium heat, sauté the garlic in oil until golden. (Do not burn the garlic or it will become bitter.)

- Add the black beans and broccolini and sauté for 1 to 2 minutes. Add the sesame oil and season with salt and pepper.

Makes 2–4 servings.

BBQ Peaches & Cream Corn on the Cob

Many people in Christian's home province of Quebec look forward to eating fresh corn on the cob cooked immediately after being picked. They take pride in cooking corn to perfection; overcooking it releases starch that makes the corn taste pasty. This recipe grills the corn in their husks. If you boil corn, do so for only 3 minutes before removing it from the salted water. This recipe uses peaches and cream corn, a variety of sweet yellow and white kernels, but of course you can use any kind.

4 cobs peaches and cream corn
2 tbsp unsalted butter
salt to taste

- Remove 1 to 2 layers of the outer leaves of the corn as well as the tassels.

- Soak the corn in water for 1 minute, so the husk won't catch on fire.

- On a barbecue on high heat, grill for 10 minutes, turning cobs over after the first 5 minutes.

- Remove from heat and open husks to eat. (You can peel the husk away and hold on to the cob while eating.) Add butter and salt to taste.

Makes 4 servings.

If you prefer to eat the corn off the cob, you can remove the kernels easily with a knife.

ROASTED ROOT VEGETABLES

On a cold evening in winter, these roasted vegetables are earthy and simple to prepare. Use any combination of vegetables that weighs a total of 2 ½ to 3 lbs (1.1 to 1.4 kg) before cooking.

4 small potatoes, skins on
2 large carrots, peeled
1 to 2 parsnips, peeled
1 sweet potato or yam, peeled
1 small turnip, peeled
1 small onion, peeled and quartered
3 cloves garlic, whole
4 to 5 tbsp olive oil
1 tbsp fresh rosemary, finely chopped
¾ tsp coarse salt
½ tsp pepper

- Preheat oven to 400°F (200°C).

- Chop the potatoes, carrots, parsnips, sweet potato, and turnip into 1-inch pieces (2.5-cm).
  In a large bowl, toss vegetables with the onions, garlic, oil, rosemary, salt, and pepper.

- Place on a baking tray and roast for 35 to 45 minutes, or until vegetables are tender and start
  to caramelize.

Makes 6 servings.

BABY ORGANIC CARROTS WITH GINGER, CHIVES & MINT

We often forget just how good carrots can be especially when they are in season. We get not only orange, but yellow and red carrots from the farm to serve at the Tomato. Carrots are best stored in the coldest part of the refrigerator and without the leafy tops.

1½ lbs (750 g) baby organic carrots
2 tbsp ginger, sliced
1 tbsp olive oil
1 tsp fresh chives, chopped
1 tsp fresh mint, chopped
salt and freshly ground pepper to taste
2 tbsp pomegranate seeds

- In a pot of boiling salted water, cook the carrots for 5 minutes until tender but still a bit crunchy.
- In a frying pan on low heat, sauté the ginger in oil for 2 minutes.
- Add the carrots, chives, and mint and sauté for 1 minute. Season with salt and pepper and add the pomegranate seeds just before serving.

Makes 4 servings.

Some people consider pomegranates messy and time-consuming, but they are worth it. The outer skin of a pomegranate is tough, leathery, and a deep-pink-to-rich-red color. The interior is separated into compartments by cream-colored (and bitter) membrane walls. These compartments have sacs filled with juicy red and pink pulp. In each sac, there is an angular, tiny red seed, which has a sweet, tart flavor. They make a beautiful garnish for both savory and sweet foods and a great addition to any salad or carrot dish.

Ginger or gingerroot is a knobby tuber with smooth tan skin. It has a pungent, spicy, sweet flavor that is wonderful in both savory and sweet dishes. An easy way to peel the gingerroot's outer skin is with the tip of a spoon.

ROASTED SIEGLINDE POTATOES

The fertile Pemberton Valley in British Columbia is known for its seed potatoes. A small family-run farm there grows many varieties of certified organic potatoes: no pesticides, herbicides, or chemical fertilizers. We support our local farms and serve these Sieglinde potatoes on our dinner menu. You can find many interesting varieties of organic potatoes at your local farmer's markets.

1 lb (500 g) Sieglinde or fingerling potatoes, chopped in half
2 tbsp olive oil
coarse salt and freshly ground pepper to taste
2 tsp fresh rosemary leaves, chopped

- Preheat oven to 400°F (200°C).

- In a large bowl, toss the potatoes in the oil, coarse salt, and pepper.

- In an ovenproof frying pan on medium heat, sauté the potatoes for 2 to 3 minutes, then place pan in the oven and roast for 30 to 35 minutes, until potatoes are golden brown.

- Sprinkle with fresh rosemary and additional salt to taste.

Makes 4 servings.

BUTTERMILK MASHED POTATOES

Mashed potatoes are the ultimate in comfort food. We use Russets because they are high in starch and low in moisture. They make light and fluffy mashed potatoes, and the buttermilk adds a tangy flavor.

2 lbs (1 kg) Russet potatoes, peeled and quartered
½ cup buttermilk
2 tbsp unsalted butter
salt and white pepper to taste

- In a pot of boiling salted water, cook the potatoes for 15 to 20 minutes, until tender.
- Drain well, then mash the potatoes (or use a food mill), adding in the buttermilk, butter, salt, and pepper until well combined.

Makes 4 servings.

There are three categories of potatoes:

1. Starchy potatoes, like Russets and purple Peruvian, which are used for mashed potatoes.

2. Waxy potatoes, which are low in starch and high in water content, like red and Yellow Finn, which are excellent for gratins.

3 All-purpose potatoes, like Yukon Gold and fingerling.

Rigatoni with Chorizo (page 83)

Bouillabaisse du Pacifique (page 80)

BBQ Peaches & Cream
Corn on the Cob (page 108)

Oven-Roasted Asparagus with Pine Nuts
& Shaved Parmesan Cheese (page 101)

CAULIFLOWER, CORN & TOASTED ALMOND SUCCOTASH

In this dish, the mild flavor of cauliflower works well with sweet corn off the cob and the texture and crunch of toasted almonds. Instead of white cauliflower, you could try pale chartreuse green cauliflower or smaller purple cauliflower (which will turn green when cooked). Fresh cauliflower should have no brown spots when purchased, and the shorter the cooking time, the better the flavor.

1 medium cauliflower, cut into small florets
2 fresh corn on the cob, husked
1 tbsp butter
¼ cup buttermilk
¼ cup sliced almonds, toasted (see note)
salt and freshly ground pepper to taste

- In a pot of boiling salted water, cook the cauliflower for about 8 minutes until tender. Drain and set aside. Once cooled, lightly mash.

- In a pot of boiling salted water, cook the corn for 3 minutes. Allow the corn to completely cool, then slice the kernels from the cob. Return corn to the pot over low heat and stir in the butter.

- Add the mashed cauliflower to the corn. Pour in the buttermilk and mix well.

- Sprinkle with toasted almonds and season with salt and pepper just before serving.

Makes 4 servings.

To toast almonds: place on a baking tray in a 350°F (180°C) oven for 4 to 5 minutes, or until brown.

Brussels Sprouts with Chili Orange Maple Butter

Brussels sprouts, which look like small cabbages, are widely available in the cold winter months and have a sweet nutty flavor. Smaller Brussels sprouts are sweeter than large ones.

1 lb (500 g) Brussels sprouts
1 tbsp olive oil
1 tbsp maple syrup or liquid honey
juice of 1 orange (2 tbsp)
½ tsp orange zest
½ tsp chili powder
salt and freshly ground pepper to taste
¼ cup pumpkin seeds, toasted (see note)

- Preheat oven to 400°F (200°C).

- Trim the Brussels sprouts by removing the outer leaves and cutting a small "x" in the stems to help them cook evenly.

- In a small bowl, combine the oil, maple syrup, orange juice and zest, and chili powder. Reserve 1 ½ tbsp of the liquid.

- Toss the Brussels sprouts in the liquid and season with salt and pepper.

- Place on a baking tray and roast for 35 to 40 minutes, until tender.

- Drizzle the reserved liquid over the Brussels sprouts and sprinkle with the pumpkin seeds before serving.

Makes 4 servings.

To toast pumpkin seeds: place on a baking tray in a 350°F (180°C) oven for about 10 minutes, or until brown.

Winter Squash

Winter squash comes in all shapes and sizes. Many people are intimidated by squash, but once you try cooking with them, you'll be glad you did.

Acorn squash is small and oval-shaped with a dark green, ribbed outer skin and orange flesh. They are sweet with a hint of a nutty flavor, and are most commonly cooked by cutting in half, removing the seeds, and then baking with a small amount of brown sugar and dot of butter. When the squash is cooked, you can eat the flesh directly out of the skin.

Blue Hubbard squash can grow very large, weighing up to 30 pounds. They have skins that are thick and bumpy with a blue hue and pale orange flesh. Look for these squash sold cut and wrapped in pieces in the produce section. They have an intense "squash" flavor, so they are good mashed or puréed for soup.

Butternut squash has a smooth texture with a sweet, nutty flavor. They're shaped like pears with flesh-to-camel-colored outer skins and orange inner flesh. Butternut squash is good baked or steamed.

Delicata is a long oblong squash with thin, yet slightly tough, edible skin that is cream-colored with green stripes. It has a fine-textured golden flesh that is sweet, nutty, and creamy tasting. This squash can be cut in half lengthwise and baked skin side down.

Kuri squash has the appearance of an oblong pumpkin with thick orange-colored skin. It has firm flesh with a delicate, mellow flavor. Kuri squash can be baked, puréed for soups, and is perfect for pies.

Spaghetti squash is shaped like a watermelon with a creamy yellow outer skin. When baked, the spooned-out flesh becomes translucent yellow strands that resemble spaghetti, hence the name. This squash has a very mild taste that works well with a sauce.

Butternut Squash & Yukon Gold Potato Gratin

This gratin is simple to bake, and the layers of potato and butternut squash, topped with cheese, make it a flavorful side dish. Butternut squash has a mildly sweet and creamy, nutty flavor. The all-purpose Yukon Gold potato has yellow flesh and a rich flavor.

2 large Yukon Gold potatoes, peeled (about 1 ½ lbs)
½ large butternut squash, peeled and seeded
½ cup heavy cream, 33% milkfat
1 tsp salt
½ tsp freshly ground pepper
1 clove garlic, minced
1 tsp of fresh herbs of your choice, finely chopped (e.g., oregano, thyme or chives)
½ cup Parmigiano-Reggiano cheese, freshly grated

- Preheat oven to 400°F (200°C).

- Using a very sharp knife, slice the potatoes and butternut squash into ⅛-inch (3-mm) thick slices.

- Grease the bottom and sides of an 8 × 8-inch (20 × 20-cm) baking pan and sprinkle about 2 tbsp of the heavy cream on the bottom.

- In the greased pan, layer the vegetables. Start with the potatoes, covering the bottom by overlapping the slices. Season with salt and pepper and dash with another tbsp heavy cream.

- Repeat process with the butternut squash. Continue layering until potatoes and squash are all used, ending with potatoes. Sprinkle with finely chopped herbs.

- Cover with foil and bake in the oven for 1 hour, then remove foil and sprinkle with grated cheese. Bake for an additional 15 minutes, or until the cheese is melted and starts to brown.

- To serve, cut into squares.

Makes 4 servings.

A lighter cream (10% milkfat) can be used instead of heavy cream. Milk doesn't work in this recipe, though; it needs the higher fat content of cream to help bind the ingredients and thicken it as it cooks.

An easy and safe way to thinly slice potatoes is to cut a piece off the bottom so that the potato sits flat on the surface of the cutting board and does not move around as you slice.

PARMESAN RICOTTA POLENTA

Polenta is a dish that originated in Northern Italy. In some regions, polenta is made with a very finely ground yellow cornmeal, and in other regions the cornmeal is the coarse variety we use in this recipe. The process is the same for both, but the end results may vary; the coarsely ground cornmeal—also known as corn grits—produces a thick polenta, and the finer cornmeal, which is yellow or pale white, makes a thinner one. Polenta can be served as a first course or a side dish, or even at breakfast time.

¾ cup heavy cream, 33% milkfat
1¼ cup water
½ tsp salt
½ cup coarsely ground cornmeal
3 tbsp ricotta cheese
3 tbsp Parmesan cheese, grated
1 tbsp butter
1 tbsp dried oregano
freshly ground pepper to taste

- Preheat oven to 400°F (200°C).

- In a medium pot on high heat, bring the heavy cream, water, and salt to a boil.

- Reduce heat and simmer. Gradually add the cornmeal, whisking constantly to avoid lumps. Continue to stir with a wooden spoon until the mixture is thick, for 3 to 4 minutes.

- Remove from heat and stir in the ricotta, grated Parmesan, butter, oregano, and pepper.

- Grease a 8 × 8-inch (20 × 20-cm) baking pan and spread the polenta over the bottom of the pan. Bake for 20 minutes.

- Cut into squares and serve hot.

Makes 4 servings.

WILD MUSHROOM RISOTTO

Our mushroom supplier, Tyler Gray of Mikuni Wild Harvest, delivers right to our kitchen door. He brings many unique and delicious cultivated mushrooms, such as Trumpet Royale (a.k.a. French Horn or King Oyster), as well as wild chanterelles, morels, porcini, and hedgehogs, to name a few. You can use any favorite in-season mushroom to make this risotto. For the rice, visit your local Italian market and purchase a high quality Italian short grain rice called Arborio, which comes in three varieties: Vialone, Carnaroli, and Baldo; each one has slightly different cooking times, texture, and grain size. The high starch content creates the creamy texture. The better the quality of rice and mushrooms, the more expensive it will be, but the end result will be worth it!

4 to 6 cups chicken stock
1 cup wild mushrooms, cleaned and sliced
3 tbsp olive oil
½ cup onion, finely chopped
1 clove garlic, minced
2 cups Arborio rice
1 cup white wine
2 tbsp butter
½ cup Parmesan cheese, grated
salt and freshly ground pepper to taste

- In a medium pot on medium heat, bring stock to a simmer.

- In a frying pan on medium-high heat, sauté the mushrooms in oil until tender and then set aside.

- In the same frying pan on medium-high heat, sauté the onions and garlic, stirring constantly until onions are translucent.

- Reduce heat to medium, add the rice and cook for about 2 minutes. (You don't want to brown the rice, just coat it with the oil.)

- Add the wine and stir until it is absorbed, then pour in the simmering stock ½ cup at a time, stirring constantly until the stock is absorbed. (This step will take about 20 minutes, and the rice will be tender but firm to the bite.)

- Once the rice is almost ready, stir in the butter and Parmesan cheese. Just before serving, add the sautéed mushrooms. (Adding the mushrooms in the last stage prevents the risotto from turning grayish in color.) Season with salt and pepper. Top with more Parmesan if desire.

Make 4–6 servings.

Mushrooms should be stored in a cool, dry place, preferably with air flow. If the mushrooms have a high amount of moisture, store them in a paper bag which will suck some of the moisture from them.

CAPELLINI NOODLES TOSSED IN SCALLION PARSLEY OIL

Capellini noodles, which are very fine, also are known as angel hair pasta. This dish, which uses scallion oil, is perfect with fish. We serve it at the Tomato with the Pan-Seared Scallops (page 53), but you can serve it with any white fish.

½ lb (250-g) capellini noodles
¼ cup Scallion Parsley Oil (page 126)
salt and freshly ground pepper to taste

- In a large pot of boiling salted water, cook the capellini noodles until al dente (cooked but still firm to the bite), about 4 to 6 minutes.
- Transfer to a large bowl and toss with the Scallion Parsley Oil until well mixed. Season with salt and pepper.

Makes 4 servings.

CORN RELISH

This relish goes great with the corn cakes (page 55) or as an accompaniment to chicken.

1 cup fresh or frozen corn niblets (see note)
¼ cup celery, finely diced
¼ cup red bell pepper, seeded and finely diced
¼ cup onion, finely diced
⅔ cup vinegar
2 tbsp sugar
2 ½ tsp cornstarch
1 tsp fresh or dry ginger
1 tsp Dijon mustard
½ tsp turmeric

- In a medium pot, combine all the ingredients and bring to a boil.

- Reduce heat and simmer for 5 minutes, or until it thickens.

- Cool before serving.

- This relish keeps in the refrigerator for up to 1 week.

Makes 1 ½ cups.

If using fresh corn, boil on the cob for 3 minutes before slicing kernels. If using frozen, thaw before using.

Dressings, Sauces & Spreads

Roasted Shallot Vinaigrette

Toasted Sesame Vinaigrette

Maple Balsamic Vinaigrette

Scallion Parsley Oil

Peppercorn Aïoli

Homemade Mayonnaise

Light Curry Mayonnaise

Red Pepper Mayonnaise

Tartar Sauce

Germaine's Tomato Fruit Ketchup

BBQ Sauce

Quick Weekday Tomato Sauce

Walnut Hummus

Traditional Basil Pesto

Chocolate Mint & Pistachio Pesto

Chipotle Butter

Saffron Rouille

Pear Chutney

Well-made sauces, dressings, and spreads are the foundation of any good kitchen. We offer suggestions here on how to use them, but feel free to be creative. For instance, you will want to serve the Quick Weekday Tomato Sauce (page 134) with the Best Ever Meatballs (page 87), but a friend of ours serves this sauce on its own on pasta.

Many of the dressings can be used on your favorite salads. What a treat it is to have a homemade condiment on hand, one in which all the ingredients are top quality, flavorful, and free of any additives.

Be creative too with the ingredients themselves. For example, try peaches instead of pears in the Pear Chutney (page 140). We use the Traditional Basil Pesto (page 136) in the Asparagus, Feta & Pesto Tart (page 54), but you can also use it on pasta, a sandwich, or a burger. And the Chocolate Mint & Pistachio Pesto (page 137) works well with lamb, venison, and halibut. Like these pestos, all of the recipes in this chapter are exceedingly versatile. I hope that you will use them as a springboard for your own ideas.

ROASTED SHALLOT VINAIGRETTE

We use this flavorful vinaigrette for the Potato-Crusted Pacific Salmon (page 77).

6 whole shallots, peeled
1 tsp canola oil
1 tsp Dijon mustard
⅓ cup red wine vinegar
1 cup extra-virgin olive oil
salt and freshly ground pepper to taste

- Preheat oven to 350°F (180°C).

- In a small ovenproof frying pan on medium heat, sauté the shallots in oil until golden brown, about 3 to 4 minutes.

- Place pan in oven for 10 minutes until the shallots become soft and tender. Remove from oven and let cool.

- In a blender or food processor, combine the shallots, Dijon mustard, and red wine vinegar. Slowly add the olive oil while continuing to blend until emulsified (see note). Season with salt and pepper.

- This vinaigrette will keep in the refrigerator for 2 weeks.

Makes 1 ½ cups.

Emulsifying is the process of combining two liquids which generally do not mix easily, to create a smooth consistency.

Toasted Sesame Vinaigrette

At the café, this thick, creamy dressing is served with Christian's Summer Salad with Local Corn, Arugula & Feta Cheese (page 40).

2 tbsp extra-virgin olive oil
2 tsp toasted sesame oil
1 tbsp Dijon mustard
1 tsp balsamic vinegar

- In a small bowl, whisk together all the ingredients until emulisfied.
- This vinaigrette will keep in the refrigerator for 2 weeks.

Makes ¼ cup.

MAPLE BALSAMIC VINAIGRETTE

The Westcoaster Salad (page 41), which uses this vinaigrette, has become one of the Tomato's signature dishes.

5 tbsp balsamic vinegar
1 tsp Dijon mustard
3 tbsp pure maple syrup
freshly ground pepper to taste
1 cup olive oil

- In a small bowl, whisk together the balsamic vinegar, Dijon mustard, maple syrup, and pepper, then slowly add the oil while continuing to whisk until emulsified.
- This vinaigrette will keep in the refrigerator for 2 weeks.

Makes 1 ½ cups.

SCALLION PARSLEY OIL

Another great oil, we use this with the Lemon-Peppered Pacific Halibut (page 79) and Capellini Noodles (page 119).

6 green onions (stalks only), chopped in 1-inch pieces
1 cup Italian parsley leaves
1 cup olive or canola oil

- In a large pot of boiling salted water, blanch the green onions and parsley until tender, about 20 to 30 seconds, then immediately place in a bowl of ice water to stop the cooking.

- Drain the parsley and onions, squeezing the excess water out. In a blender or food processor, combine parsley and onions with the oil and blend for 2 to 3 minutes.

- Using a fine mesh strainer, remove the pulp from the parsley and green onions.

- This oil will keep in the refrigerator for 4 to 5 weeks.

Makes 1 cup.

Buy a squeeze bottle from a kitchen shop to store your scallion oil for easy use when cooking.

Blanching helps the onions and parsley retain their color.

PEPPERCORN AÏOLI

Aïoli is a classic French sauce not unlike a mayonnaise. We serve this peppery variation with the Crab Cakes with Dungeness and Blue Crabmeat (page 51).

2 cloves garlic
1 tsp sea salt
1 large egg
1 egg yolk
1 cup olive oil
¼ tsp pink peppercorns, crushed

- In a blender or food processor, combine the garlic and salt. Add the egg and egg yolk and blend well. Slowly add the oil while continuing to blend until emulsified, then add the peppercorns.
- This aïoli will keep in the refrigerator for 3 to 4 days.

Makes 1 cup.

Pink peppercorns are not true peppercorns but the dried berries of the Baies Rose plant. They are pungent and slightly sweet, and can be freeze-dried or packed in water or brine.

HOMEMADE MAYONNAISE

Serve this mayonnaise with the Tomato-Style Fish & Chips (page 82), and on sandwiches like the Tomato Fresh Food Café Heirloom BLT Sandwich (page 66), the Vegetarian Sandwich (page 67), and the Montreal Corned Beef Reuben (page 72). It's also the base for our Red Pepper Mayonnaise (page 130), which we use in our other sandwiches and burgers, and our Tartar Sauce (page 131).

1 large egg
1 tsp Dijon mustard
1 tsp fresh lemon juice
½ tsp salt
pinch of cayenne
1 cup canola oil

- In a blender or food processor, combine all the ingredients except the oil. Slowly add the oil while continuing to blend until emulsified. Taste and adjust seasoning if necessary.

- This mayonnaise will keep in the refrigerator for up to 1 week.

Makes 1 ½ cups.

LIGHT CURRY MAYONNAISE

We use this slightly spicy mayo on the Moroccan Turkey Burger (page 74).

◇ 2 tbsp Homemade Mayonnaise (page 128)
◇ 1 tbsp Dijon mustard
◇ 1 tsp sherry vinegar or apple cider vinegar
◇ 1 tsp Madras curry

- In a bowl, whisk all the ingredients together.
- This mayonnaise will keep in the refrigerator for up to 1 week.

Makes ¼ cup.

This is a versatile mayo that we also use on the Tomato To Go Three-Cheese & Basil Panini (page 68), the Italian Countryside Sandwich (page 70), the Italian Panini (page 71), and the Portobello Burger (page 73).

RED PEPPER MAYONNAISE

1 small red bell pepper, grilled
½ cup Homemade Mayonnaise (page 128)
pinch of cayenne

- To grill a red bell pepper, char it on the grill or under the broiler until the skin becomes blackened. Place it inside a zip-lock plastic bag and let it cool for about 20 minutes.

- Remove the skin and seeds, then in a blender or food processor, combine the pepper, mayonnaise, and cayenne and blend until smooth.

- This mayonnaise will keep in the refrigerator for up to 4 or 5 days.

Makes ¾ cup.

TARTAR SAUCE

This is the tartar sauce we use for the Tomato-Style Fish & Chips (page 82).

1 cup Homemade Mayonnaise (page 128)
1 tbsp sour cream
1 tbsp Dijon mustard
1 tbsp dill pickle, finely chopped
1 tbsp capers, rinsed and finely chopped
1 green onion, finely chopped
1 tbsp parsley, finely chopped
zest of 1 lemon
juice of ½ a lemon
salt and pepper to taste

- In a medium bowl, combine all the ingredients.
- This sauce will keep in the refrigerator for 1 week.

Makes 1 ½ cups.

GERMAINE'S TOMATO FRUIT KETCHUP

Christian's mom Germaine makes this ketchup at the end of summer from the harvest of tomatoes and fruits from local orchards. It's an interesting combination that makes a deliciously chunky ketchup. It's a fine accompaniment to halibut and other white fish, but in winter it's perfect with French Canadian Tourtière (page 56). If you make this in winter, when peaches are out of season, use an extra pear in place of the peach.

5 medium tomatoes, cubed
1 peach, cubed
1 medium apple, cubed
1 pear, cubed
1 medium onion, diced
⅓ cup yellow bell peppers, seeded and diced
½ cup white sugar
⅓ tsp salt
3 tbsp apple cider vinegar
⅓ cup white vinegar
1 tsp pickling spice, tied up in a cheesecloth bag

- In a large pot on high heat, combine all the ingredients. Bring to a boil, then reduce heat and simmer for 1 ½ hours.

- Remove from heat and let cool before using. Remove cheesecloth containing pickling spice.

- This ketchup will keep in the refrigerator for 1 week.

Makes 3 cups.

BBQ Sauce

This is the sauce for Chef's Baby Back Ribs (page 90), perfect for an outdoor feast.

½ red onion, finely diced
6 cloves garlic, chopped
¼ cup butter
12 plum tomatoes, diced
½ cup ketchup
6 tbsp molasses
2 tbsp Worcestershire sauce
¼ cup Dijon mustard
¼ cup brown sugar
¼ cup honey
2 tsp cayenne pepper
6 tbsp ancho chili pepper
2 tsp paprika

- In a large pot on medium heat, sauté the onions and garlic in the butter for 5 minutes until soft.

- Add the tomatoes and sauté for an additional 5 minutes. In a medium bowl, combine the remaining ingredients and add to the pot.

- Reduce heat and simmer for 30 minutes, stirring often to prevent sticking to the bottom of the pot. Remove from heat and cool mixture slightly. In a blender or food processor, blend until smooth.

- This sauce will keep in the refrigerator for 4–5 days.

Makes 2 cups.

QUICK WEEKDAY TOMATO SAUCE

During winter when tomatoes aren't that flavorful, it's okay to use a good quality, organic canned tomato sauce. This recipe is quick, simple, and versatile, and uses a mix of organic canned sauce and fresh tomatoes; serve it with the Best Ever Meatballs (page 87).

1 medium onion, chopped
2 cloves garlic, chopped
1 tbsp olive oil
3 large Roma tomatoes, chopped
1 28-oz (796-ml) can organic tomato sauce
salt and freshly ground pepper to taste

- In a large saucepan on medium heat, sauté the onions and garlic in oil for 5 minutes.
- Add the tomatoes and cook for an additional 2 minutes, then add the canned sauce and season with salt and pepper.
- Reduce heat to low and simmer for another 10 minutes.
- This sauce will keep in the refrigerator for 4–5 days.

Makes 2 cups.

WALNUT HUMMUS

A great-tasting hummus, we spread it on our popular Vegetarian Sandwich (page 67). Tahini is a paste made from ground sesame seeds.

1 14-oz (398-ml) can chickpeas (garbanzo beans), drained and rinsed
1 clove garlic
juice of 1 large lemon
⅓ cup tahini
¼ tsp salt
2–3 tbsp olive oil
¼ tsp pinch of cayenne
⅓ cup water
⅓ cup walnuts

- In a food processor, blend together all the ingredients until smooth.
- This hummus keeps in the refrigerator for 1 to 2 weeks.

Makes 1 ½ cups.

Walnuts are harvested in California September through November; there are 37 varieties grown there. Four varieties—Chandler, Hartley, Payne, and Serr—account for over 80% of total production. Walnuts are one of the most widely consumed nuts in the world. Inside the tough shell, its curly nutmeat has a rich, sweet flavor.

TRADITIONAL BASIL PESTO

Freshly picked basil is the very essence of summer. Its beautiful scent and incredible flavor add a punch to late summer and fall recipes. In winter, frozen pesto can be added to a quick pasta dish and adds zest to the Asparagus, Feta & Pesto Tart (page 54).

3 cloves garlic
2 cups fresh basil leaves
⅓ cup extra-virgin olive oil
¼ toasted pine nuts
¼ cup grated Parmesan cheese
½ tsp salt
½ tsp freshly ground pepper

- In a blender or food processor, combine the garlic and basil. Slowly add the oil while continuing to blend until emulsified.

- Scrape down the sides of the bowl and add the pine nuts, cheese, salt, and pepper. Process until well-blended.

- This pesto can be stored in the refrigerator for up to 1 week. You can also freeze it for several months.

Makes 1 cup.

CHOCOLATE MINT & PISTACHIO PESTO

Recently, on one of our first deliveries of the summer, Susan Davidson of Glorious Garnish and Seasonal Salad Company brought us a bag of freshly cut chocolate mint. Coincidentally, We had just returned from Hawaii and brought back some macadamia nuts. Chef James had a great idea: make a chocolate mint macadamia nut pesto to serve with lamb. When they went to make the dish, they realized that Sous-Chef Joe had eaten all the nuts the night before. In the spirit of teamwork, Ben, one of the cooks, suggested they use pistachios instead. The result is this awesome pesto, guaranteed to be a hit with chocolate lovers. Although we used it on lamb, you can try it on venison or halibut too.

1 cup chocolate mint leaves, packed (see note)
1 cup Italian parsley, packed
4 cloves garlic
½ cup shelled pistachio nuts, toasted
¼ cup Parmesan cheese, freshly grated
2 tbsp extra-virgin olive oil
2 tbsp hazelnut oil
1 tsp salt
½ tsp freshly ground pepper

- In a blender or food processor, combine the chocolate mint, parsley, garlic, nuts, and cheese until mixture is finely chopped.

- Slowly add in both oils while continuing to blend until emulsified. Season with salt and pepper.

- This pesto can be stored in the refrigerator for up to 1 week. You can also freeze it for several months.

Makes ¾ cup.

There are over 30 different types of mint available, the most common of which are spearmint and peppermint. Chocolate mint, as you can guess, has a subtle chocolate flavor; it's available at farmer's markets, and the plants themselves are easily found in garden centers. Chocolate isn't the only unusual type of mint; there's also applemint and pineapple mint, which are usually used to garnish beverages. Once mint is picked, store it in a plastic bag in the vegetable crisper of your refrigerator. If you can't find chocolate mint, use spearmint.

CHIPOTLE BUTTER

Compound butters, also called flavored butters or "specialty" butters, are easy to prepare and make a great addition to any meal. Take a ½ cup of unsalted butter at room temperature and blend it in a food processor with your favorite herbs, spices, and peppers. Or mix honey or maple syrup with your favorite nut to make a great compound butter for pancakes and waffles. This chipotle butter adds flavor to the Grilled Beef Tenderloin (page 86). Make extra and keep it in the freezer until it's needed.

½ cup unsalted butter, at room temperature
3 tbsp canned chipotle peppers
½ shallot, diced
1 tbsp parsley, chopped
¼ tsp coriander
¼ tsp fresh oregano, chopped
¼ tsp ancho chili powder or any good quality chili

- In a blender or a food processor, combine all the ingredients until well blended.
- Transfer the butter to a piece of plastic wrap and roll to form a 4-inch (10-cm) log.
- Wrap tightly and refrigerate until firm, about 2 hours.
- This butter will keep in the freezer for up to 1 month.

Makes a 4-inch (10-cm) log.

Chipotle peppers are dried, smoked jalapeños. They can be purchased dried, pickled, or canned in adobo sauce.

Variations:

Lemon and Dill Butter: ½ cup unsalted butter, zest of 1 lemon, and 1 tbsp fresh dill, chopped.

Sun-Dried Tomato Butter: ½ cup unsalted butter, ¼ cup sun-dried tomatoes, 2 tbsp fresh basil, chopped, and ½ tsp capers, drained and rinsed.

Wine and Sage Butter: ½ cup unsalted butter, 1 tbsp white wine, and ¼ cup fresh sage, chopped.

Maple Syrup Butter: ½ cup unsalted butter, ⅓ cup maple syrup, and ⅓ cup toasted hazelnuts, chopped.

SAFFRON ROUILLE

A rouille is a sauce that is traditionally served on toasted baguette slices to accompany fish soups. This one is made with saffron, for use in the Bouillabaisse du Pacifique (page 80).

4 cloves garlic
2 large eggs
2 egg yolks
2 oz reduced bouillabaisse broth (see note)
2 cups olive oil
pinch of coarse salt
pinch of saffron threads

- In a blender or food processor, combine the garlic, eggs, egg yolks, and reduced broth.

- Slowly add the oil while continuing to blend until emulsified. (It will be thick.)

- Stir in the saffron threads.

Makes 1 ½ to 2 cups.

To reduce bouillabaisse, take 4 oz (100 g) of broth and reduce by one-half.

Saffron is the most expensive spice in the world. Why? Because saffron threads are from the stamen of the purple crocus flower, and there are only three of them per flower. The good news is that it takes a very little amount to create lots of flavor.

PEAR CHUTNEY

This chutney goes great with the Braised & Grilled Long Bone Pork Chops (page 91).

3 Bosc pears, diced
¼ cup red onion, diced
¼ cup red bell pepper, seeded and diced
2 tsp jalapeno peppers, seeded and diced
1 tsp fresh garlic, minced
⅓ cup sugar
½ cup apple cider vinegar
1 tsp mustard seeds
1 tsp coriander seeds
½ cinnamon stick

- In a medium pot over high heat, combine all the ingredients. Bring to a boil, then reduce heat and simmer for 30 to 40 minutes until thickened.

- This chutney should be made the day before you use it. Once made, it will keep in the refrigerator for up to 1 week.

Makes 3 cups.

Baking

Tomato Café's Popular Whole Wheat Bread

Rosemary Parmesan Focaccia

Deliciously Sticky Cinnamon Buns

Cheddar Cheese Scones

Oatmeal Maple Scones

White Chocolate, Orange & Raspberry Scones

Doug's Banana Blueberry Bran Muffins

Mocha Hazelnut Muffins

Pumpkin Streusel Muffins

Our Big Double Chocolate Espresso Cookies

Hazelnut Praline Biscotti

Shortbread Two Ways:
My Mom Carell Spilos's Shortbread
Anne Kelly's Scottish Shortbread

Tomato To Go Chocolate Rice Crispies

Carrot Coconut Loaf with
Cream Cheese Frosting

I started baking with my mom when I was a young child. To me, the warm smells of something baking in the oven are powerful reminders of home. When I brought friends back to our house after school, we'd all sit down at the kitchen table, and my mother would make us toast using her homemade bread. We'd slather the thick slices with peanut butter and often didn't stop until we ate the entire loaf.

There's nothing like taking something you've baked out of the oven and serving it to friends and family, showing them that you care. The wholesomeness of the Tomato Café's Popular Whole Wheat Bread (page 143) comes from using oat flakes, bran, and three different seeds. Our Rosemary Parmesan Focaccia (page 144) offers different combinations of cheese and fresh herb toppings. Cookies and biscotti are year-round "sweet things," good for picnic baskets in summer and as gifts at Christmas.

Making muffins and scones is simple and economical when you use seasonal fruits and fresh nuts. Doug's Banana Blueberry Bran Muffins (page 149) are popular with many of the Tomato's customers as well as Doug himself, and the White Chocolate, Orange & Raspberry Scones (page 148) are great with seasonal berries.

We hope these recipes inspire you to bake at home—it's worth the effort!

Pastry chef Jennifer Lee.

TOMATO CAFÉ'S POPULAR WHOLE WHEAT BREAD

We make this whole wheat bread daily (and in large batches) at the Tomato. It's so popular that people ask for the recipe (and for their breadbaskets to be refilled). We use it for sandwiches too.

2 ¼ cups warm water (105°–115°F/40–45°C)
2 tbsp blackstrap molasses
2 tbsp active dry yeast
⅓ cup brown sugar
3 cups whole wheat flour
1 ½ cups all-purpose flour
1 cup large oat flakes
½ cup oat bran
1 tbsp salt
⅓ cup olive oil
⅓ cup sunflower seeds
⅓ cup flax seeds
⅓ cup sesame seeds

- In the bowl of an electric mixer, combine the warm water, molasses, yeast, and sugar. Let sit for approximately 6 minutes until the yeast starts to foam.

- Add the flours, oat flakes, oat bran, salt, and oil and combine in the mixer using a dough hook on medium speed for about 10 minutes. Add the seeds and mix on low speed until well incorporated, about 5 minutes.

- Divide the dough in half and shape into rounds. Place each round in a large oiled bowl. Cover with a cloth or plastic wrap and place in a warm area until the doughs double in size, about 1 to 1 ½ hours.

- Punch the doughs down and reshape into rounds. Place on a baking tray lined with parchment paper and let rest covered until it doubles in size again, about 2 hours.

- Preheat oven to 400°F (200°C).

- Using a sharp knife, cut three slashes in the top of each loaf. Bake for 35 to 45 minutes, until golden brown.

- To test for doneness, knock on the bottom crust; it should sound hollow when done.

Makes 2 round loaves.

ROSEMARY PARMESAN FOCACCIA

This focaccia is made daily in our bakery and used for our panini sandwiches. Be creative with your toppings, matching herbs and cheeses like the traditional rosemary and Parmesan, basil and Asiago, or oregano and feta. You can also use Summer-Roasted Roma Tomatoes (page 99) or roasted garlic and mozzarella.

2 tbsp active dry yeast
2 tbsp granulated sugar
2½ cups warm water (105°–115°F/40°–45°C)
6 cups all-purpose flour
2 tsp salt
¼ cup olive oil
2 tbsp coarse salt
¼ cup fresh rosemary, chopped
½ cup fresh Parmesan cheese, grated

- In the bowl of an electric mixer, combine the yeast, sugar, and warm water. Let sit until yeast starts to foam, about 6 minutes. Add the flour, salt, and oil and combine in the mixer with a dough hook on low speed for about 10 minutes.

- Form dough into a rectangular shape. Let rest for 5 minutes, then on a lightly floured surface, roll it out to fit an oiled 13 × 17½-inch (33 × 30-cm) baking pan. Press the dough into the pan and brush the top with oil. Let rest in a warm place uncovered, until the dough rises to the rim of the pan, about 45 minutes.

- Dimple the top of the dough with your fingers. Sprinkle with the coarse salt, rosemary, and cheese.

- Preheat oven to 350°F (180°C).

- Let the dough rest again until it rises slightly above the rim of the pan, about 30 minutes.

- Bake for 30 minutes, or until golden brown.

Makes 1 loaf.

The leaves of the rosemary plant resemble fine evergreen needles. Rosemary can be harvested either during or after flowering, when the leaves are most aromatic. It can be used in soups, sauces, and marinades, and in stews with lamb or poultry. It also adds flavor to salads and breads.

Roasted Sieglinde Potatoes (page 111)

Breakfast drinks (page 31-32)

Peach Blueberry Galette (page 172)

Tomato To Go Chocolate Rice Crispies (page 156)

DELICIOUSLY STICKY CINNAMON BUNS

These buns are deliciously sticky, hence their name. If you are lucky enough to live where nuts are local and plentiful, use them. But these days most markets have a great variety of nuts to choose from, whether they're fresh Macadamias from the Hawaiian Islands, pecans from the South, or walnuts from California.

Glaze:

- 2 cups packed brown sugar
- ½ cup honey
- ⅔ cup butter
- 1 tbsp cinnamon
- ⅓ cup whipping cream, 33% milkfat

- ½ cup chopped nuts, toasted (for topping)

Dough:

- 2 tsp active dry yeast
- ¼ cup warm water
- 3½ cups all-purpose flour
- 2 tsp salt
- 2 tbsp honey
- ⅓ cup oil
- ⅔ cup warm water
- 1 large egg

For the glaze:

- In the bowl of an electric mixer, combine the first 4 ingredients, then add the whipping cream and mix well.

For the dough:

- In the bowl of an electric mixer, combine the yeast and warm water. Let stand for about 6 minutes until mixture starts to foam. Add the flour and salt, then the remaining ingredients and combine, with the dough hook on medium speed, for about 10 minutes.

- Transfer the dough to an oiled bowl and cover with a cloth or plastic wrap. Let the dough rise for 1½ hours, or until it doubles in size.

- Grease a 13 × 9-inch (33 × 22-cm) metal baking pan and spread 1½ cups of the glaze over the bottom of the pan.

- When the dough has doubled, punch it down. On a lightly floured surface, roll it out into an 8 × 12-inch (20 × 30-cm) rectangle.

- Spread a thin layer of glaze on top of the dough right to the edges.

- Roll the dough up into a log, starting at a long side. Using a serrated knife, cut the log into 8 equal pieces. Place each piece, cut side down, into the baking pan on top of the glaze.

- Cover and let rise until they double in size, about 1 hour.

- Preheat oven to 350°F (180°C).

- Bake for 30 to 35 minutes or until the tops are golden brown.

- Remove from the oven and immediately transfer the buns onto a cookie tray. Top with toasted chopped nuts of your choice.

Makes 8 buns.

CHEDDAR CHEESE SCONES

These scones are one of the first things I ever learned to make with my mom. When I was young, she inspired me to love using my hands to create wonderful baked goods. I remember sitting in front of the oven and watching and smelling the scones as they baked, waiting excitedly to eat them hot. My mom gave me three tips on making them: combine the ingredients together until just mixed; if you use salted butter, omit the additional salt; and be patient while they're in the oven to let them bake to a golden brown.

4 cups all-purpose flour
2 tbsp baking powder
1 tsp salt
¾ cup cold, unsalted butter, cubed
2 cups medium cheddar cheese, grated
1⅓ cups milk
½ cup medium cheddar cheese, grated (for topping)

- Preheat oven to 375°F (200°C).

- In a large bowl or food processor, combine the flour, baking powder, and salt, and mix well. Cut in the butter and mix until it resembles peas.

- With a spatula, mix in the grated cheese, then the milk, until blended.

- On a lightly floured surface, knead the dough until smooth, and then roll out into a disk 1 ½ inches (3¾ cm) tall.

- Using a 3-inch (7 ½-cm) round cutter, cut scones and place on a baking tray. Top each scone with a thin layer of cheddar cheese.

- Bake for 30 to 35 minutes, or until golden brown.

Makes 8 scones.

OATMEAL MAPLE SCONES

Maple syrup is a sweetener made by reducing the sap of certain species of maple trees found only in North America, mainly in Quebec, New York, and Vermont. French settlers in Quebec were astonished when they first saw the aboriginals—who used the syrup as both a food and a medicine—cut slits in the maple trees to harvest the sap. Unlike honey, maple syrup must be refrigerated after opening. 100% pure maple syrup is available at most supermarkets; also look for vendors at your local farmer's market. Maple syrup and strawberries go well together, so strawberry jam on these scones is just perfect.

Scones:

- 2 ¼ cups all-purpose flour
- ½ cup rolled oats
- 1 tbsp baking powder
- 1 tbsp brown sugar
- 1 tsp salt
- 1 cup cold, unsalted butter, cubed
- ¼ cup buttermilk
- ¼ cup 100% pure maple syrup
- 2 large eggs
- 1 tsp vanilla extract

Maple Glaze:

- ⅔ cup icing sugar
- ¼ cup 100% pure maple syrup
- ½ tsp vanilla extract

For the scones:

- Preheat oven to 375°F (190°C).
- In a large bowl or food processor, combine the flour, rolled oats, baking powder, brown sugar, and salt. and mix well. Add the butter and mix until the butter resembles peas.
- In a separate bowl, combine the buttermilk, maple syrup, eggs, and vanilla and add to the flour mixture. Combine until just mixed.
- Knead the dough until smooth, then roll out into a disk 1 ½ (3 ¾ inches) tall.
- Using a 3-inch (7 ½-cm) round cutter, cut scones and place on a baking tray.
- Bake for 30 to 35 minutes, or until golden brown.

For the glaze:

- While the scones are baking, in a bowl, combine the icing sugar, maple syrup, and vanilla.
- Remove scones from the oven and let cool for about 5 minutes, then drizzle glaze on top of each scone.

Makes 6–8 large scones.

WHITE CHOCOLATE, ORANGE & RASPBERRY SCONES

In summer when raspberries are fresh, try this flavorful combination of white chocolate, orange, and raspberry. A great variation is dark chocolate and sour cherries in the same amounts.

3 cups all-purpose flour
3 tsp baking powder
¾ cup white sugar
¼ tsp salt
1 cup cold, unsalted butter, cubed
3 large eggs
1 tsp vanilla extract
⅓ cup orange juice

1 tsp orange zest
⅓ cup white chocolate, cut into
   small chunks
⅓ cup fresh or frozen raspberries
1 egg + 1 tbsp milk (for egg
   wash)
½ cup white sugar (topping)

- Preheat oven to 350°F (180°C).

- In a large bowl or food processor, combine the flour, baking powder, sugar, and salt and mix well. Add the cold butter and mix until the butter resembles peas.

- In a bowl, whisk the eggs, vanilla, orange juice, and zest. Add to the flour mixture and combine until just mixed.

- Add the white chocolate and raspberries and gently fold in with a spatula.

- On a lightly floured surface, shape the dough into a disk about 8-inch (20-cm) round and cut into 12 triangles.

- In a bowl, combine the egg and milk. Brush tops of scones with egg wash and sprinkle with white sugar.

- Bake for 40 minutes, or until golden brown.

Makes 12 scones.

You can prepare these scones, including brushing the tops with egg and sprinkling with sugar, and then freeze them until you are ready to bake. Bring to room temperature before baking.

Raspberries vary in size, but wild ones are smaller than cultivated varieties. Raspberries are fragrant and sweet and have a slightly tart taste that is more delicate than that of strawberries. When buying raspberries, choose plump fruits and avoid those that are soft and dull in color. Raspberries should not be washed; they tend to absorb the water and become soft. But if you want to wash them, do so quickly and gently just before serving. Because they are highly perishable, picked berries should not be exposed to the sun or left at room temperature for long periods of time. For longer storage, pack them loosely and keep in the refrigerator for up to 2 or 3 days.

DOUG'S BANANA BLUEBERRY BRAN MUFFINS

Every evening at the Tomato, we look forward to the arrival of Doug, our favorite customer. He has his own seat at the bar; on the back of his chair, a sign reads: "YOU GOTTA KNOW THIS IS DOUG MARSHALL'S SEAT, JULY 14, 2003, 65 YEARS YOUNG." Doug is like a father to the Tomato staff; he knows more about them than we do. His wife Barbara comes to the Tomato too, but when she's at work, Chef James and the staff take good care of him. Before his golf game on Saturday mornings, he likes to come in to have a bran muffin with blueberries. We created this recipe just for him.

2 cups all-purpose flour
¾ cup whole wheat flour
¾ cup oat bran
¾ cup wheat bran
¾ cup brown sugar
1½ tsp baking soda
¾ tsp cinnamon
¼ tsp ground nutmeg

¼ tsp salt
pinch of cardamom
3 medium ripe bananas, mashed
3 large eggs
¾ cup buttermilk
6 tbsp oil
¾ cup fresh or frozen blueberries

- Preheat oven to 350°F (180°C).

- In a large bowl, combine the first 10 ingredients.

- In a separate bowl, combine the bananas, eggs, buttermilk, and oil.

- Combine the wet ingredients with the dry until just mixed. Add the blueberries and gently fold into the batter.

- Spoon into muffin tins lined with paper cups or sprayed with cooking spray.

- Bake for 30 to 35 minutes until golden brown, and a toothpick inserted into the center of a muffin comes out clean.

Makes 1 dozen muffins.

There are over 20 varieties of blueberries native to Canada and the United States (they are rarely found in Europe). In North America, Aboriginal peoples used blueberries to season pemmican (a dried meat). Because they are easily damaged, blueberries should be washed quickly before using. To prevent them from bleeding into the batter, gently fold them into the batter at the end, and be sure not to overmix. If your fresh berries are squashed, you can freeze them and then add them to your muffin batter. They keep only for a few days in the refrigerator.

MOCHA HAZELNUT MUFFINS

These muffins are very moist, and with both coffee and chocolate as ingredients, are an alternative means of getting your caffeine fix. Hazelnuts, also known as filberts, are grown here in British Columbia; we see them at the markets for a short time in August. Also try using pecans, almonds, or walnuts in this recipe.

1 ½ cups all-purpose flour
1 ¼ cups whole wheat flour
1 cup brown sugar
⅓ cup cocoa powder, sifted
½ tsp baking powder
1 tsp baking soda
1 tsp salt
3 eggs
¾ cup olive oil
1 cup buttermilk
½ cup strong black coffee
1 tsp vanilla extract
1 cup semi-sweet chocolate chips
1 cup hazelnuts, chopped
¼ cup hazelnuts, finely chopped (for topping)

- Preheat oven to 350°F (180°C).

- In a large bowl, combine the flours, brown sugar, cocoa powder, baking powder, baking soda, and salt.

- In a separate bowl, whisk together the eggs, oil, buttermilk, coffee, and vanilla.

- Combine the wet ingredients with the dry until just mixed. Fold in the chocolate and hazelnuts.

- Spoon batter into muffin tins lined with paper cups or sprayed with cooking spray. Sprinkle top of muffins with the hazelnuts.

- Bake for 30 to 35 minutes until golden brown and a toothpick inserted into the center of a muffin comes out clean.

Makes 18 muffins.

PUMPKIN STREUSEL MUFFINS

These muffins are light, and the crumbly topping adds texture. Once you try them, you'll want to make them all year round. It's best to use canned pure pumpkin instead of fresh, which contains too much liquid. You can also add fresh, frozen, or dried cranberries to the recipe. To make a pumpkin loaf instead, bake the batter in a loaf pan for 1 hour 15 minutes at 350°F (180°C).

Streusel:

¼ cup cold, unsalted butter, cut into cubes
¼ cup sugar
6 tbsp flour
1 tsp cinnamon

Muffins:

2 cups all-purpose flour
1½ cups whole wheat flour
2½ cups light brown sugar

4 tsp baking powder
1 tsp salt
1 tbsp cinnamon
1 tsp ground nutmeg
½ tsp cloves
4 eggs
2 cups canned pure pumpkin
⅔ cup canola oil
½ cup fresh orange juice
4 tsp orange zest

- Preheat oven to 350°F (180°C).

- In a bowl of an electric mixer, combine all the streusel ingredients until the mixture is crumbly. Set aside.

- In a large bowl, combine the flours, sugar, baking powder, salt, and spices.

- In a separate bowl, whisk together the eggs, pumpkin, oil, orange juice, and zest.

- Combine the wet ingredients with the dry until just mixed.

- Spoon batter into muffin tins lined with paper cups or sprayed with cooking spray. Sprinkle tops of muffins with streusel.

- Bake for 35 minutes until golden brown and a toothpick inserted into the center of a muffin comes out clean.

Makes 18 muffins.

OUR BIG DOUBLE CHOCOLATE ESPRESSO COOKIES

This is a large, luscious, melt-in-your-mouth dark chocolate cookie with a hint of coffee, and topped with white chocolate chunks. It is our most popular cookie! Across the street at the Park Theatre, owner Leonard Schein sells these and several of our other cookies at his concession stand. They're better than popcorn!

1 cup semi-sweet chocolate chunks
⅓ cup unsalted butter
2 large eggs
⅔ cup white sugar
pinch of salt
1 tbsp ground espresso beans
1 tsp vanilla extract
1⅓ cup all-purpose flour
1 tsp baking powder
1 cup white chocolate chunks
12 white chocolate chunks (for tops of each cookie)

- Preheat oven to 325°F (160°C).

- In a small bowl over a pot of gently simmering water, melt the semi-sweet chocolate and butter. Let sit to cool to room temperature.

- In the bowl of an electric mixer with the paddle attachment, combine the eggs, sugar, salt, espresso, and vanilla. Add the chocolate mixture and continue to mix. Scrape down sides of the bowl, then add the flour and baking powder and mix until well blended.

- Fold in the white chocolate with a spatula.

- Let the batter sit for 10 minutes at room temperature. (Or, if it's a hot day, refrigerate for 10 minutes.)

- Using a 2-oz cookie scoop (or ⅓ cup each), place scoops of dough on a baking sheet and top each with a white chocolate chunk. Do not flatten dough.

- Bake for 15 to 18 minutes, or until set.

Makes 12 large cookies.

HAZELNUT PRALINE BISCOTTI

The traditional French praline is made with a combination of hazelnuts and almonds, but you can use only hazelnuts (as in this recipe) or pecans. The flecks of sweetness, as I like to call them, make these biscotti festive, great gifts for Christmas or Valentine's Day.

Praline:

- ½ cup sugar
- ¼ cup water
- ½ cup + 1 cup hazelnuts, toasted and skinned

Dough:

- ¾ cup butter
- 1 cup sugar
- 1 egg
- 1 tsp vanilla extract
- 3 cups all-purpose flour
- 2 tbsp baking powder

For the praline:

- In a saucepan on medium heat, bring the water and sugar to a boil until the sugar starts to caramelize and turn golden brown. Add the ½ cup hazelnuts. Pour the mixture onto a greased baking pan and let cool.

- Once cooled, break into pieces and place in a food processor. Add the 1 cup hazelnuts and grind into a fine powder.

For the dough:

- Preheat oven to 350°F (180°C).

- In the bowl of an electric mixer with the paddle attachment, cream the butter and the sugar together until light and fluffy. Add the egg and vanilla and mix until well-blended.

- In a separate bowl, combine the flour and baking powder, then add to the creamed mixture and mix well.

- Add the ground praline to the dough and mix until blended.

- Divide the dough into two equal pieces. On a lightly floured surface, with your hands, roll each piece into a log about 13 inches (33-cm) long and place onto a baking tray lined with parchment paper. Flatten the logs so they measure about 2 ½ to 3 inches (5 to 7 cm) wide.

- Bake for 30 minutes. Remove from oven and let cool, about 20 minutes. Reduce oven temperature to 300°F (150°C).

- Once cooled, cut the logs into ¾-inch (2-cm) slices. Return to baking tray and bake for about 30 minutes, until the biscotti are crisp.

- Cool and store biscotti in an airtight container for up to several weeks.

Makes 36 biscotti.

SHORTBREAD TWO WAYS:
MY MOM CARELL SPILOS'S SHORTBREAD

Every Christmas, I bring out my mom's shortbread recipe, and we bake batches of it to sell at the Tomato To Go. Recently, my friend Dawn Kelly and I discovered that our mothers both made shortbread cookies with the same ingredients, but using different methods. We know our mothers would love to be honored and remembered for these amazing, melt-in-your-mouth cookies.

1 cup butter
½ cup berry or baker's sugar (see note, page 155)
2 cups all-purpose flour
Pecans, almonds, or hazelnuts (for topping)

- Preheat oven to 350°F (180°C).

- In the bowl of an electric mixer using the paddle attachment, cream the butter. Gradually add the sugar and mix until light and fluffy. Add the flour and combine until just mixed.

- On a lightly floured surface, roll the dough out until it is ¼-inch thick. Using a 2-inch round crinkle cookie cutter, cut out the shortbread and place them onto a baking sheet lined with parchment paper. Place half a pecan, or an almond or hazelnut, on top of each cookie. Bake for 15 minutes, until golden brown. Store in an airtight container.

Makes 36 cookies.

For a variation, make chocolate-dipped shortbread by dipping half of each cookie into melted dark chocolate.

ANNE KELLY'S SCOTTISH SHORTBREAD

◊ 1 cup butter
◊ ½ cup berry or baker's sugar (see note)
◊ 2 cups all purpose flour

- Preheat oven to 375°F (190°C).

- In the bowl of an electric mixer with the paddle attachment, cream the butter. Gradually add the sugar and mix well. Add the flour and mix well.

- Knead the dough, then form into 2 rounds, each ½-inch thick. Crimp the edges and prick the tops with a fork.

- Place rounds on a baking sheet lined with parchment paper. Bake for 5 minutes, then reduce oven temperature to 300°F (150°C) and bake for another 45 minutes.

- While still warm, cut into wedges. Store in an airtight container.

Makes 24–28 cookies.

◊ Berry sugar (also known as baker's sugar) is extra fine granulated sugar found in the baking section of grocery stores. It measures the same as regular sugar but dissolves more quickly.

TOMATO TO GO CHOCOLATE RICE CRISPIES

These eye-catching squares sit in a large glass jar on the counter of the Tomato To Go, and neither kids nor their parents can resist them. The chocolate and candies add to the charm. The large amount of marshmallows helps to create the soft, gooey texture that everyone loves.

⅓ cup butter
7 ½ cups mini-marshmallows
2 tsp vanilla extract
10 cups rice cereal
2 to 3 cups chocolate chips
48 Smarties or M&M candies

- To keep the melted marshmallows from sticking, spray the inside of a large heavy pot and a 9 × 13-inch (33 × 23-cm) baking pan with cooking spray.

- In the large pot on low heat, stir the butter and the marshmallows with a high-heat spatula until melted.

- Remove pot from heat. Add the vanilla and mix well, then add the rice cereal and combine until well mixed.

- Spread the mixture onto the baking pan and refrigerate for 5 to 10 minutes, until it sets.

- In a small microwave-safe bowl, melt the chocolate chips in the microwave on high for 2 minutes.

- Remove the rice crispies from the pan all at once by tipping it upside down. Cut into 8 equal squares.

- Dip ½ of each square into the melted chocolate. Place on a cookie tray lined with wax paper and immediately place 6 candies on top of the chocolate end of each square.

- Refrigerate for 10 minutes to let chocolate set.

- Wrap squares individually with plastic wrap, then store in a jar or container at room temperature.

Makes 8 large squares.

High-heat spatulas, which you can find at any kitchenware store, are made to withstand the heat and do not melt at high temperatures.

CARROT COCONUT LOAF WITH CREAM CHEESE FROSTING

Carrot loaf is a good way to get carrots and their high content of vitamin A and potassium into your diet. The amount of carrots makes this loaf super moist. It's great to make year round, and the cream cheese frosting is so good, you'll be tempted to eat it on its own!

1 ⅓ cup brown sugar, packed
1 ⅓ cup vegetable oil
4 large eggs
2 cups all-purpose flour
⅔ cup fine coconut
1 tsp baking powder
1 tsp baking soda
½ tsp cinnamon
¼ tsp ground nutmeg
½ tsp salt
2 ⅔ cups carrots, grated

Frosting:

½ cup butter, at room temperature
¾ cup (6 oz) cream cheese, at room temperature
1 cup confectioner's (icing) sugar, sifted

For the loaf:

- Preheat oven to 350°F (180°C).

- In the bowl of an electric mixer with the paddle attachment, combine the brown sugar, oil, and eggs and mix well.

- In a large bowl, combine the dry ingredients, then add to the egg mixture, mixing well. Add the carrots and fold in until combined.

- Pour mixture into a 9 ½ × 5 ½-inch (24 × 14-cm) loaf pan lined with parchment paper.

- Bake for 80 to 90 minutes, or until a toothpick inserted in the middle of the loaf comes out clean. Let cool.

For the frosting:

- In the bowl of an electric mixer, cream the butter and cream cheese until smooth. Add the sifted confectioner's sugar and mix well.

- When the loaf is cooled, spread a layer of frosting on top.

Makes 1 loaf.

Desserts

Chocolate Mint Crème Brulée

Strawberry Mascarpone Cream Roulade

White and Dark-Striped Cheesecake

Hazelnut Prune Plum Tart

The Tomato's Classic Chocolate Cake with
Chocolate Espresso Frosting

Maple Syrup Peach Pie

Kristine's Pumpkin Cheesecake

Lemon Meringue Tarts

Peach Blueberry Galette

Simply Vanilla Ice Cream

Organic Belle de Boskoop Apple Pie

When Christian and his siblings were growing up, a meal without dessert was unthinkable. Their mother, Germaine Gaudreault, would serve dessert at both lunch and dinner; the kids would hide any dessert leftovers from lunch so that she'd have to make a different one at dinnertime. Christian's mother always used seasonal ingredients in her desserts and baking. That tradition has stayed with Christian all his life, and it is one I share with him. Let what fruits are in season dictate what desserts you prepare. Try specialty varieties found at farmer's markets.

Whenever possible, look for certified organic fruit, which is grown without herbicides and pesticides and without chemical fertilizers. The soil in which organic fruit trees are grown retains all essential minerals and vitamins, which makes the fruits taste better. Try the Organice Belle de Boskoop Apple Pie (page 74), which is so good with Simply Vanilla Ice Cream (page 173). Another favorite is the Maple Syrup Peach Pie (page 168), which satisfies Christian's cravings for both peaches and maple syrup, the latter a remnant of his childhood in Quebec. In winter months, when fresh fruits are not so plentiful, you can always count on chocolate desserts like the Chocolate Mint Crème Brulée (page 161), the Tomato's Classic Chocolate Cake with Chocolate Espresso Frosting (page 166), and the White and Dark-Striped Cheesecake (page 164).

CHOCOLATE MINT CRÈME BRULÉE

This Chocolate Mint Crème Brulée was made as a special order for one of our customers. She wanted to have the recipe so Ted, one of our managers who has been with us for ten years, promised her it would go into the cookbook. Here it is!

8 oz (225 g) good quality dark chocolate
3 cups heavy cream, 33% milkfat
1 cup half-and-half cream, 10% milkfat
½ cup white sugar
6 peppermint tea bags
½ cup white sugar (for egg mixture)
9 egg yolks
white sugar (to caramelize)

- Preheat oven to 325°F (160°C).

- In a double boiler on medium heat, melt the chocolate. Remove from heat and set aside to cool.

- In a heavy saucepan on high heat, bring the heavy cream, half-and-half cream, ½ cup sugar, and tea bags to a boil. Remove from heat and let tea bags steep for 15 minutes.

- In a bowl, whisk together the second ½ cup sugar and egg yolks until just mixed.

- Remove the tea bags and temper the egg mixture by gradually adding the cream mixture to the eggs, whisking continuously. (Tempering prevents the eggs from scrambling.)

- Whisk in the melted chocolate, and then strain. Let the mixture sit for 15 minutes then use a ladle to skim off any bubbles.

- In a roasting pan, arrange 8 ramekins. Pour the mixture into each ramekin. Pour boiling water into the roasting pan, being careful not to get any into the ramekins. Cover the roasting pan with foil and bake for 25 minutes, or until the custards are set.

- Remove ramekins from the pan and cool to room temperature. Refrigerate until ready to serve.

- Just before serving, sprinkle a very thin layer of white sugar on the top of each one. Use a kitchen blow torch or place under the broiler in the oven to caramelize the tops.

Makes 8 servings.

STRAWBERRY MASCARPONE CREAM ROULADE

Pastry Chef Jennifer Lee is young, energetic, and very talented. She gets to be creative and adventurous at the Tomato because the dessert list changes every week. Our desserts differ between lunch and dinner and reflect the seasonal and local fruit we receive. Jennifer always has great ideas for incorporating fruit; when the local strawberries were in season, she created this amazing roulade, which is like a sophisticated strawberry shortcake: rich, creamy filling inside a light sponge cake combined with ripe, juicy strawberries.

Cake:

8 large egg whites
¼ cup white sugar
½ tsp cream of tartar
8 large egg yolks
pinch of salt
½ cup white sugar
½ tsp pure vanilla extract
⅓ cup vegetable oil or unsalted butter
¾ cup all-purpose flour, sifted

Filling:

1 cup whipping cream,
   33% milkfat
¼ cup confectioner's (icing) sugar
1 tsp pure vanilla extract
1 cup mascarpone cheese,
   at room temperature
2 cups fresh strawberries, sliced

For the cake:

- Preheat oven to 325°F (160°C).

- In the bowl of an electric mixer with the whisk attachment, whisk the egg whites until frothy, then add the sugar and cream of tartar slowly, continuing to whisk until stiff peaks are formed. Transfer to another bowl and set aside.

- In the bowl of an electric mixer with the whisk attachment, whip the egg yolks, salt, sugar, vanilla, and oil until the ribbon stage is reached (see note). Gently fold in the flour by hand. Fold in the egg whites.

- Line a 17½ ×13-inch (44 × 33-cm) jelly roll pan with parchment paper. Spread filling evenly into the pan with an offset spatula.

- Bake for 30 to 35 minutes, until cake bounces back when you touch it with your finger. Remove from oven and let cool.

For the filling:

- In the bowl of an electric mixer with the whisk attachment, whip the cream, sugar, and vanilla until stiff. Transfer to another bowl and set aside.

- In the bowl of an electric mixer with the paddle attachment, soften the mascarpone cheese; do not overmix or the cheese will split and become grainy.

- With a rubber spatula, fold in the whipped cream in two additions, making sure to scrape down the bowl each time. Mix until smooth.

- To make the roulade, remove the cooled cake from the jelly roll pan. Flip the cake over and spread the filling on the underside of the cake. Place the sliced strawberries on top and roll up horizontally.

- Refrigerate for 2 hours. Trim off edges and slice into 10 pieces.

Makes 10 servings.

The ribbon stage is when egg yolks and sugar are beaten until they are light yellow in color and very thick. When the mixture is lifted with a whisk, the batter falls back into the bowl in a ribbon-like trail.

Strawberries grow in temperate zones all over the world. Wild strawberries are small and juicy and have a more concentrated flavor than cultivated varieties (of which there are over 500). Like most berries, look for shiny, firm fruit with a healthy color (a dull color usually means it's overripe). Just before using strawberries, rinse them quickly so that they can't absorb excess water and hull the green calyx before using.

WHITE AND DARK-STRIPED CHEESECAKE

This cheesecake is as good to look at as it is to eat. It's hard to believe it works, but it does; just follow the directions. To everyone's surprise, it comes out looking like zebra stripes or a bull's eye. Kids love it!

Crust:

1½ cups chocolate crumbs

⅓ cup butter, melted

White filling:

1½ lbs (750 g) cream cheese, softened at room temperature

1 cup white sugar

3 large eggs

2 tsp pure vanilla extract

Dark filling:

1½ lbs (750 g) cream cheese, softened at room temperature

1 cup white sugar

3 large eggs

2 tsp pure vanilla extract

7 oz (200 g) dark chocolate, melted

⅓ cup water, at room temperature

For the crust:

- Preheat oven to 325°F (160°C).

- Grease a 9-inch (23-cm) or 10-inch (25-cm) springform pan and line the bottom with parchment paper.

- In a small bowl, combine the chocolate crumbs and melted butter. Press into the bottom of the pan and halfway up the sides.

- Bake for 10 minutes. Remove from oven and cool.

For the fillings:

- Preheat oven to 325°F (160°C).

- For the white filling: in a food processor, mix the softened cream cheese until smooth, then add the sugar and mix. Add the eggs and vanilla, combining until just mixed. Transfer to a jug with a spout.

- For the dark filling: in a food processor, mix the softened cream cheese until smooth. Add the sugar and blend again, then the eggs and vanilla, and combine until just mixed. In a separate bowl, stir together the water and melted chocolate, then add to the cream cheese mixture and mix. Transfer to another jug with a spout.

- Pour ⅓ of the dark filling into the middle of the crust. Next, pour ⅓ of the white filling on top of the dark in the middle of the pan. Continue until all the filling is used. At this point, you will have a striped circular pattern.

- Bake for 1 hour and 25 minutes, or until just set. During the last 15 minutes, if necessary, loosely tent a piece of foil over the cheesecake to keep the white filling from browning.

- Remove from oven and cool to room temperature, then refrigerate overnight before serving.

Makes 12 servings.

HAZELNUT PRUNE PLUM TART

This mouth-watering dessert has a rich, buttery shortbread crust with a crumbly hazelnut filling, topped with sweet ripe prune plums.

Shortbread crust:

- 1½ cups all-purpose flour
- ½ cup confectioner's (icing) sugar, sifted
- 1 tbsp cornstarch
- 1 cup butter, softened

Filling:

- ⅓ cup white sugar
- ½ cup hazelnuts, finely ground
- ½ cup all-purpose flour
- ½ cup cold, unsalted butter
- 1½ lbs fresh prune plums, stones removed
- 1 tbsp white sugar (for sprinkling)
- ¼ cup apricot glaze or jam

For the crust:

- Preheat oven to 350°F (180°C).

- In a small bowl, sift together flour, confectioner's sugar, and cornstarch. Set aside. In the bowl of an electric mixer with the paddle attachment, cream the butter, then add the sifted ingredients and mix until it comes together.

- With your hands, press the dough into a 10-inch (25-cm) tart pan. Prick pastry bottom with a fork. Chill for 1 hour before baking. Line with parchment paper and weigh down the bottom of the tart with uncooked beans to avoid shrinkage.

- Parbake for 20 to 25 minutes, or until the crust is set. Remove from oven and set aside.

For the filling:

- In a small bowl, combine the sugar, ground hazelnuts, flour, and butter and fill the crust with the mixture.

- Cut the plums into quarters and arrange the slices in a circle overlapping (the plums will shrink during baking). Sprinkle sugar on top. Bake for 35 to 40 minutes, or until the plums are soft.

- Before serving, warm the apricot glaze or jam and brush on top of the plums.

Makes 14 servings.

When buying plums, look for fruits that have a pleasant scent and yield to the slight pressure of your finger. Ideally, the skin should have a powdery bloom, a sign that it has not been over-handled. Plums can be left out at room temperature if unripe, but check frequently as they ripen quickly. Ripe plums will keep in the refrigerator for a few days.

THE TOMATO'S CLASSIC CHOCOLATE CAKE WITH CHOCOLATE ESPRESSO FROSTING

My mom never used cake mixes; she always baked from scratch. The texture of this cake is light and chocolatey, and the frosting is very rich. It's good with ice cream and a large cold glass of milk.

Cake:

- 2 cups cake flour, sifted
- 1½ tsp baking soda
- ¼ tsp salt
- ¼ cup shortening
- ¼ cup unsalted butter
- 2 cups white sugar
- ¾ cup cocoa powder, sifted
- ¾ cup hot water
- 2 large eggs
- 1 tsp pure vanilla extract
- 1 cup buttermilk

Frosting:

- 1 cup butter
- 2 cups confectioner's (icing) sugar
- 1½ cups cocoa
- ¼ cup milk
- ¼ cup espresso, or strong coffee
- 1 tsp pure vanilla extract

For the cake:

- Preheat oven to 350°F (180°C).

- Lightly grease 3 9-inch (23-cm) cake pans and line with parchment paper.

- In a large bowl, sift the flour, baking soda, and salt together and set aside.

- In the bowl of an electric mixer with the paddle attachment, cream the shortening and butter until light and fluffy. Add the sugar and sifted cocoa powder and mix well.

- Slowly add the hot water, stopping to scrape down the sides of the mixing bowl when needed.

- Add the eggs one at a time until blended, then the vanilla. Alternately, add the buttermilk and dry ingredients, starting and ending with dry ingredients. The dry ingredients will be added in 3 additions; the buttermilk in 2.

- Divide the batter equally into the 3 cake pans.

- Position the rack in the lower third of the oven. Bake for 30 to 35 minutes. When done, the cake will shrink away from the sides of the pan, and a toothpick inserted into the center will come out clean.

- Let the cakes cool in the pans for 15 minutes, then remove and place onto a cooling rack.

For the frosting:

- In the bowl of an electric mixer with the paddle attachment, cream the butter until light and fluffy.

- In a bowl, sift together the cocoa powder and confectioner's sugar. Add to the butter and mix well, scraping down the sides of the bowl when needed. Slowly add the milk, espresso, and vanilla. Mix until fluffy, about 5 minutes. The frosting will lighten in color as the consistency becomes soft and easy to spread.

- When cooled completely, place the first cake layer onto a serving plate or cake board, flat side down and coat with frosting. Repeat with remaining 2 layers. After assembling the cake, frost the sides. You can also add chocolate shavings to the sides of the cake.

Makes 14–16 servings.

Four helpful tips:

1. Before frosting the cake, place strips of wax or parchment paper under the bottom of the cake to keep the plate clean. Remove when frosted.

2. To make chocolate curls, use a vegetable peeler and shave from a block of room-temperature chocolate.

3. Refrigerate the cake after frosting so the layers do not slide around, then serve at room temperature.

4. If the cake layers have a dome-like top, trim them to make them even so the frosting stays on and cake layers don't slide off.

MAPLE SYRUP PEACH PIE

Make this pie when peaches are in season. The smell of the juicy, fragrant fruit baking in the oven will make your mouth water.

Pastry:

- 2 cups all-purpose flour
- 2 tsp white sugar
- 1 tsp salt
- ¾ cup cold, unsalted butter, cut into small cubes
- 1 large egg
- ¼ cup ice water
- 2 tsp vinegar

Filling:

- ¼ cup packed light brown sugar
- 3 tbsp flour
- 1 tsp ground cinnamon
- ¼ tsp nutmeg
- 8 cups fresh peaches, peeled and sliced
- ¼ cup pure maple syrup
- 1 tbsp white sugar plus 1 tbsp milk (for top of crust)

- In a food processor, pulse together the flour, sugar, salt, and butter until the mixture resembles peas.

- In a bowl, mix together the egg, ice water, and vinegar. Add to the food processor and pulse until dough comes together. By hand, shape the dough into 2 equal disks, cover with plastic wrap, and refrigerate for at least 2 hours, or overnight.

- In a large bowl, stir together the brown sugar, flour, cinnamon, and nutmeg. Stir in the peaches and maple syrup and set aside.

- Remove pastry dough from refrigerator. Roll out the first disk to fit a 10-inch (25-cm) pie pan with a little overhang. Roll out the other disk to a 12-inch (30-cm) circle for the top crust. Pour filling into bottom crust and cover with top crust. Seal with water and crimp the edges

- Brush the top with milk and sprinkle with sugar. Cut slits in the top of crust. Chill for at least half an hour before baking.

- Preheat oven to 425°F (220°C).

- Bake the pie in the lower third of the oven for 25 to 30 minutes. Reduce temperature to 375°F (190°C) and continue baking for another 25 to 30 minutes, or until the crust is golden brown and the filling is bubbling.

- Cool on a wire rack to room temperature for 2 hours before serving.

Makes 8–10 servings.

Peaches spoil very easily even when unripe, so it is best to buy only the quantity you need and use them as soon as possible. When buying, choose fragrant fruits that are unblemished and not too hard. Peaches will keep for only 3 to 4 days at room temperature.

KRISTINE'S PUMPKIN CHEESECAKE

Kristine, one of our managers, created this cheesecake. A nice garnish for this is the Maple Syrup Candied Pecans from the Poached Pear & Pecan Salad (page 44).

Crust:

1½ cups graham crumbs

⅓ cup butter, melted

½ cup toasted pecans, finely chopped

Filling:

½ lb (225-g) cream cheese, softened at room temperature

½ lb (225-g) mascarpone cheese, softened at room temperature

1 cup white sugar

1½ cups canned pure pumpkin

½ cup sour cream

1 tsp cinnamon

1 tsp nutmeg

1 tsp ground ginger

⅛ tsp cloves

3 large eggs

½ cup white sugar (to caramelize)

For the crust:

- Preheat oven to 325°F (160°C).

- Grease a 9-inch (23-cm) springform pan and line bottom with parchment paper.

- In a small bowl, combine the graham crumbs, melted butter, and pecans. Press the mixture into the bottom of the pan and halfway up the sides.

- Bake for 10 minutes. Remove from oven and set aside to cool.

For the filling:

- Preheat oven to 325°F (160°C).

- Using an electric mixer or a food processor, mix the softened cream cheese and mascarpone cheese until smooth, then add the sugar and mix.

- Add the pumpkin purée, sour cream, cinnamon, nutmeg, ginger, and cloves and combine until mixed.

- Add the eggs one at a time, combining until just mixed.

- Pour into crust and bake for 1 hour 15 minutes, or until set.

- Remove from oven and cool to room temperature, then refrigerate overnight before serving.

- To serve, cut cheesecake into slices, sprinkle each slice with sugar, and use a kitchen blowtorch to caramelize. This must be done with each individual slice because you cannot cut through the sugar once it has caramelized.

Makes 12 servings.

LEMON MERINGUE TARTS

This recipe is for my editor Melva, who loves lemon meringue tarts. It uses Italian meringue which according to Mel, gives these tarts the "wow" factor. If you prefer, you can serve them without the meringue, using fresh berries of your choice for the topping instead.

Shortbread Crust:

1½ cups all-purpose flour
½ cup confectioner's (icing) sugar, sifted
1 tbsp cornstarch
1 cup butter, softened

Meringue:

⅓ cup water
1 cup sugar
5 large eggs whites
¼ cup sugar (for egg mixture)

Lemon Curd:

6 large egg yolks
¾ cup white sugar
zest and juice of 3 large lemons
¾ cup cold butter, cut into small cubes

For the crust:

- Preheat oven to 350°F (180°C).

- In a small bowl, sift together the flour, confectioner's sugar, and cornstarch. Set aside.

- In the bowl of an electric mixer with the paddle attachment, cream the butter, add the sifted ingredients, and mix until it comes together.

- With your hands, press the dough into 8 individual 4-inch (10-cm) tart pans. Prick pastry bottoms with a fork. Chill for 1 hour before baking.

- Bake for 20 minutes, or until the crusts are set and golden brown.

For the lemon curd:

- In a stainless steel bowl, whisk together the egg yolks and sugar, then add the lemon juice and zest.

- Place the bowl over a pot of boiling water and whisk constantly until mixture thickens, about 15 minutes.

- Remove from the heat and whisk in the cold butter, a few pieces at a time.

- Place plastic wrap directly on top of the curd to prevent a skin from forming. Refrigerate until cool.

- Spread into the individually baked tart shells until mixture is level with the crust.

For the meringue:

- In a pot on high heat, bring water and 1 cup sugar to a boil. Using a candy thermometer, check until the sugar mixture reaches 230°F (110°C).

- In the bowl of an electric mixer with the whisk attachment, whip the egg whites with ¼ cup sugar to medium peaks.

- When sugar and water mixture reaches 240°F (115°C), slowly pour it into the egg whites. (240°F is the called "soft ball stage"; which is the temperature of sugar syrup used in Italian meringues.) Whip mixture until it is completely cooled and forms stiff peaks, about 20 minutes with the electric mixer.

- Using a piping bag with a star tip, pipe the meringue onto the tarts in peaks.

- Refrigerate until ready to serve. Just before serving, use a kitchen blowtorch to lightly brown the meringue tips.

Makes 8 4-inch (10-cm) tarts.

Although these tarts are best served the same day, you can make the crust and the lemon curd ahead of time, even the day before. Assemble when ready to serve.

PEACH BLUEBERRY GALETTE

This rustic-style free-form tart is simple to make and offers a fabulous way to use summer fruit. The pastry is tender and buttery, and the filling speaks of the sweet, juicy flavor of peaches combined with firm, plump blueberries.

Pastry:

1 ½ cups all-purpose flour
1 tsp white sugar
¼ tsp salt
½ cup unsalted butter, frozen and cut into
    ½-inch (1-cm) cubes
¼ cup ice water

Filling:

2 tbsp all-purpose flour
6 tbsp white sugar
5 large ripe peaches, peeled and
    cut into ½ inch (1 cm) slices
¾ cup fresh blueberries
2 tbsp white sugar (for sprinkling)
confectioner's (icing) sugar
    (for dusting)

For the pastry:

- Preheat oven to 400°F (200°C).

- In a food processor, pulse the flour, sugar, salt, then add the butter and mix for 25 seconds, or just until the mixture resembles coarse crumbs.

- Add the ice water and mix for 15 seconds until blended. The mixture will still be crumbly.

- Remove from the food processor bowl and knead the dough by hand then form into a flat disk.

- On a lightly floured surface, using a rolling pin, roll into a 12-inch (33-cm) circle. Place on a baking sheet and refrigerate.

For the filling:

- Preheat oven to 350°F (180°C).

- While the pastry is chilling, in a large bowl combine the flour and sugar. Add the peaches and blueberries and gently combine.

- Place the filling in the middle of the pastry, leaving a 3-inch (7-cm) margin around the edge. Allow the pastry to warm up slightly, then fold the pastry edges over the fruit and pleat pastry to make a circle. If any cracks appear, seal them to prevent juices from running out during baking. Brush the pastry edges with cold water and sprinkle with 2 tbsp sugar.

- Bake for 45 to 50 minutes, or until the crust is golden brown and the filling is bubbling.

- Cool for 20 minutes. Before serving, dust the edges with confectioner's sugar.

Makes 12 servings.

In place of peaches and blueberries, you could substitute 5 cups plums and 1 cup raspberries, or 5 cups apples and 1 cup cranberries.

SIMPLY VANILLA ICE CREAM

There are many types of ice cream makers for home use, from hand churning to electric machines. If you like ice cream, it's worth having an ice cream maker; you can add a handful of just-picked strawberries or other seasonal fruit from the garden to this basic recipe.

2 cups whole milk
1 ½ cups whipping cream, 33% milkfat
½ cup white sugar
1 vanilla bean, split lengthwise and seeds scraped
½ cup sugar
10 egg yolks

- In a large pot, heat the milk, whipping cream, sugar, and vanilla bean and seeds. Bring to a boil, then reduce heat.

- In a medium bowl, whisk together the sugar and egg yolks.

- Gradually add hot milk mixture to yolks, whisking continuously. (This will temper the eggs, to prevent them from scrambling.)

- Place back into the pot on stove on medium heat and bring liquid to 180°F (82°C), measuring the temperature with a candy thermometer and stirring constantly, until thick enough to coat a spoon.

- Strain and place in freezer until cold, preferably overnight.

- Churn according to the instructions on your ice cream maker.

Makes 4 cups.

ORGANIC BELLE DE BOSKOOP APPLE PIE

Belle de Boskoop apples are a Dutch heirloom variety. During fall apple season, we get these from Glorious Garnish and Seasonal Salad Company, Susan Davidson's farm in Aldergrove, BC. When Jennifer Lee, the Tomato's pastry chef, started using these apples to make our apple pie, customers returned in droves to have "just one more piece" served with our Simply Vanilla Ice Cream (see page 173). You can substitute Granny Smith apples for this recipe, or if you can find them, try late season Mutsu apples, also known as Crispin, which are a cross between a Golden Delicious and Indo.

Pastry:

2 cups all-purpose flour
1 tsp salt
2 tsp white sugar
¾ cup cold unsalted butter, cut into
    small cubes
1 large egg
¼ cup ice water
2 tsp vinegar

Filling:

10 to 12 cups organic apples,
    peeled and cut into eighths
    (about 12 apples)
½ cup white sugar
½ cup brown sugar
1 tsp cinnamon
¼ tsp nutmeg
¼ tsp cloves
¼ tsp ginger
¼ cup butter
zest and juice of 1 lemon
3 tbsp cornstarch
2 tbsp cold water

For the pastry:

- In a food processor, pulse together the flour, salt, sugar, and butter until the mixture resembles peas.

- In a bowl, mix together the egg, ice water, and vinegar.

- In a food processor, combine the egg and flour mixtures and pulse until dough just comes together (less than 10 seconds). By hand, shape the dough into 2 equal disks, cover with plastic wrap, and refrigerate for at least 2 hours, or overnight.

For the filling and pie:

- Preheat oven to 400°F (200°C).

- In a large pot on high heat, cook the apples, both sugars, spices, butter, lemon juice and zest for 15 to 20 minutes, or until most of the liquid is evaporated.

- In a small bowl, mix together the cornstarch and cold water, then add to the apple mixture. Cook until mixture boils, plus 1 additional minute. Remove from heat and spread apples on a pan to cool.

- Remove pastry dough from refrigerator. Roll out the first disk to fit a 10-inch (25-cm) pie pan with a little overhang. Roll out the other disk to a 12-inch (30-cm) circle for the top crust.

- Pour cooled filling into bottom crust, then cover with top crust. Seal with water and crimp the edges.

- Brush the top with 1 tbsp milk and sprinkle with sugar. Cut slits in the top of crust. Chill for at least half an hour before baking.

- Bake in the lower third of the oven for 20 minutes, then reduce temperature to 350°F (180°C) and bake for another 30 to 40 minutes, or until the crust is golden brown and the filling is bubbling.

- Cool on a wire rack to room temperature for 2 hours before serving.

Makes 8–10 slices.

There are nearly 8,000 varieties of apples grown worldwide. They generally ripen either in late summer or fall. "Summer apples" are good for eating as is, while "fall apples" are most often used for cooking or baking. The degree of acidity of the sugar content also determines which apples are good for what purpose:

- Firm, crisp, and juicy apples for eating right off the tree.

- Drier and sweeter (but slightly acidic) apples for baking.

- Barely ripe apples, which will be high in pectin for jams and jellies.

- Sweet apples that hold their shape for applesauce.

Aimee Watson of Glorious Garnish and Seasonal Salad Co.

White and Dark-Striped Cheesecake (page 164)

Hazelnut Prune Plum Tart (page 165)

Lemon Meringue Tarts (page 170)

The Tomato's Classic Chocolate Cake
with Chocolate Espresso Frosting (page 166)

INDEX

Breakfast

Breakfast Scramble 19

Buttermilk Cornmeal Pancakes 28

Christian's Tomato, Red Pepper,
Asparagus & Gruyere Frittata 22

Crispy Bacon, Gruyere & Spinach
Quiche 24

Dave's Blackberry Mascarpone
French Toast with Caramelized
Apples 27

French Breakfast 29

Poached Eggs on English Muffins
with European Back Bacon 21

Sun-dried Cranberry Pecan
Granola 30

Three Cheese Strata 25

Tofu Scramble & Salsa 26

Tomato, Chorizo & Manchego
Frittata 23

Yogurt Cheese 28

Zucchini & Eggplant Omelet 20

Broccoli

Broccolini with Crispy Garlic &
Fermented Black Beans 107

Brussels sprouts

Brussels Sprouts with Chili Orange
Maple Butter 114

Burgers

Moroccan Turkey Burger 74

Portobello Burger 73

Buttermilk

Buttermilk Cornmeal Pancakes 28

Buttermilk Mashed Potatoes 112

Cakes

The Tomato's Classic Cake with
Chocolate Espresso Frosting 166

Carrots

Baby Organic Carrots with Ginger,
Chives & Mint 110

Carrot Coconut Loaf with Cream
Cheese Frosting 157

Cauliflower

Cauliflower, Corn & Toasted Almond
Succotash 113

Chard, Swiss

Spinach & Swiss Chard
Cannelloni 96

Cheese

Breakfast Scramble 19

Three-Cheese Strata 25

Tomato To Go Three-Cheese Basil
Panini 68

Cheese, bocconcini

Italian Countryside Sandwich 70

Italian Panini 71

Tomato, Bocconcini, Basil & Red
Onion Salad 35

Cheese, cheddar

Cheddar Cheese Scones 146

Cheese, chèvre

Poached Pear & Pecan Salad with
Warm Goat Cheese 44

Cheese, feta

Asparagus, Feta & Pesto Tart 54

Christian's Summer Salad with Corn,
Arugula & Feta Cheese 40

Heirloom Tomato Salad 37

Oven-Roasted Tomatoes & Feta on
Crostini with Infused Basil Oil 48

Cheese, Gruyère

Christian's Tomato, Red Pepper,
Asparagus & Gruyère Frittata 22

Crispy Bacon, Gruyère & Spinach
Quiche 24

Zucchini & Eggplant Omelet 20

Cheese, manchego

Tomato, Chorizo & Manchego
Frittata 23

Cheese, mascarpone

Dave's Blackberry Mascarpone
French Toast with Caramelized
Apples 27

Strawberry Mascarpone Cream
Roulade 162

Cheese, Parmesan

Oven-Roasted Asparagus with
Pine Nuts & Shaved Parmesan
Cheese 101

Parmesan Ricotta Polenta 117

Rosemary Parmesan Focaccia 144

Cheesecakes

Kristine's Pumpkin Cheesecake 169

White and Dark-Striped
Cheesecake 164

Chicken

Free-Range Chicken Breasts in a
Tarragon Mustard Marinade 84

My Sister's Chicken Noodle Soup 63

Oven-Roasted Lemon Rosemary
Chicken 85

Oven-Roasted Lemon Rosemary
Chicken Sandwich 69

Chickpeas (*see beans – chickpeas*)

Chives

Baby Organic Carrots with Ginger,
Chives & Mint 110

Chocolate

Chocolate Mint Crème Brulée 161

Our Big Double Chocolate Espresso
Cookies 152

The Tomato's Classic Cake with
Chocolate Espresso Frosting 166

Tomato To Go Chocolate Rice
Crispies 156

Chocolate, white

White Chocolate, Orange &
Raspberry Scones 148

ABOUT THE AUTHORS

CHRISTIAN GAUDREAULT spent his childhood in Quebec, Canada, where he helped in his family's restaurant. He has worked in Asia, Europe and in Vancouver (with chef and restaurateur Umberto Menghi as well as Yves Veggie Cuisine) before becoming a partner, then co-owner with wife Star Spilos, of the Tomato Fresh Food Café.

STAR SPILOS's lifelong interest in food and in baking began by watching her mother create luscious desserts. A graduate of the Dubrulle French Culinary School, she received a Les Dames d'Escoffier scholarship to the Culinary Institute of America – Napa Valley. In addition to co-owning the Tomato, she teaches at David Thompson Secondary School in Vancouver.

THE TOMATO FRESH FOOD CAFÉ

3305 Cambie Street (at West 17th Avenue), Vancouver, BC Canada

Tel: 604-874-6020 | Fax: 604-871-6881 | Tomato to Go: 604-873-4697

info@tomatofreshfoodcafe.com | www.tomatofreshfoodcafe.com